Understanding the Workings of Faith

By
Pastor/Teacher James L. Monteria

CLM Publications & Publishing, LLC
P.O. Box 932
Chesterfield, VA 23242

Understanding the Workings of Faith

All rights reserved. No part of this book may be reproduced without written permission from the publisher except for use of brief review for further of the Kingdom of God unless otherwise indicated, all Scriptures are taken from the King James Version of the Bible

CLM Publications, LLC

P.O. Box 932

Chesterfield, VA 23832

www.clmpublication.info

ISBN: 978-0-9821450-8-1

Cover Design/Graphics: Shelly E. Middleton

Author: James L. Monteria

Associate Editor: Paulette Scott

Published by CLM Publications, LLC

Copyright © 2011 by CLM Publications & Publishing, LLC, Printed in the United States of America; All rights reserved under International Copyright Law. Contents and cover may not be reproduced in whole or in part in any form without the expressed written consent of the publisher.

Table of Contents

INTRODUCTION	PAGE 1
1. What does it mean to be a person of faith?	PAGE 3
2. How do we get the God kind of faith?	PAGE 13
3. Faith, the Operation of God	PAGE 20
4. Activating the Power of God through Faith	PAGE 25
5. Faith and Belief are not the Same!	PAGE 30
6. The Enemies of Faith	PAGE 38
7. The Law of Faith	PAGE 43
8. Faith is your Servant PT1	PAGE 53
9. Faith is your Servant PT2	PAGE 67
10. Examples: Individuals Possessing STRONG Faith	PAGE 83
11. How to make your Servant Faith Strong	PAGE 104
12. We must see Faith as a lifestyle	PAGE 120
13. daily Faith Confession	PAGE 128
Scriptures References	PAGE 136
To receive Jesus Christ as your own personal Lord and Savior	PAGE 134
Endnotes	PAGE 140
About the Author	PAGE 141

Acknowledgement

First, and foremost, I would not even know God, or be able to write anything about Him, were it not for His grace and mercy! I have come to appreciate the grace of God, the Lordship of Jesus Christ, and the Holy Spirit's presence in my life and my ministry, even more than words could express.

Foreword

Come and Learn of Me - In sharing the message of Jesus, according to Matthew 11:28-30; states that Jesus said "Come unto me, all ye that labor and are heavy laden, and I will give you rest. Take my yoke upon you, and learn of me; for I am meek and lowly in heart: and ye shall rest unto your souls. For my yoke is easy, and my burden is light."

To be a successful co-laborer in the things of God, it is necessary to know what the ground rules are so that we can flow with the Spirit of God. It is through faith that we have access to the wonderful blessings that our loving Heavenly Father has for us to enjoy while here on earth. It is very essential that we are to *Understanding the Workings of Faith*; therefore this book offers insight, examples, and practical illustrations on this topic and in how to make FAITH work! This book will help you walk in the victory that our loving Heavenly Father has so wonderfully provided for us.

UTWOF Table of Contents

Faith is the Master Key

• • •

It is through faith that we activate and access the things that our loving Heavenly Father has provided for us to enjoy in the here and now!

Faith is the currency of the Kingdom, if you want anything in the kingdom it must be access by faith

. . .

Introduction

I am sharing in this book with you as a pastor; my objective is to help you to have a greater understanding about Faith. When sharing with you about faith, I am not talking about what use to be on job application, meaning what faith are you: Protestant, Catholic, or Jew? I will be sharing an enormous amount of scriptures on the subject of Faith that can be applied to the Christian life.

As a pastor I teach on many different subjects, because there is a need for faith in all subjects. See Salvation, being born-again is just the beginning.

In this book I will be sharing about the kind of Faith that moves the hand of God. What I am talking about is the Faith of the Bible. The kind of faith that Jesus used when he quailed the storm, the kind of faith that Jesus used when he raised the dead, the kind of faith that Jesus used when he ministered to the sick, the kind of faith that Jesus used when he cast out demons. The kind of faith that God has give unto every believer based on Romans 12:3. I trust that you understand what is meant when I say…"the kind of Faith that moves the hand of God."

Why is it so imperative that we understand the workings of Faith?

To be a successful co-laborer in the things of God, it is necessary to know what the ground rules are so that we can flow with the Spirit of God. It is through faith that we have access to the wonderful blessings that our loving Heavenly Father has for us to enjoy while we are here on earth.

It is very essential that we are to **_Understanding the Workings of Faith_**; therefore this book offers insight, examples, and practical illustrations on this topic and how to make FAITH work!

This book will help you walk in the victory, which our loving Heavenly Father has so wonderfully provided for us.

How do we activate or access the things that God, our Heavenly Father, has provided for us?

It is through faith that we activate or access the things that our loving Heavenly Father has provided for us to enjoy in the here and now!

Faith is the currency of the Kingdom of God, if you want anything in the Kingdom it must be access by faith.

Faith is the Activator

As we familiarize ourselves with the Bible, the Word of God, we know that it is faith that makes the Bible work for you. The things (Scriptures) in the Bible don't work because they are in the Bible. It works because you have faith in it. You put it to work by faith.

> Romans 10:17; *"Faith comes by hearing and hearing The Word of God."*

1. What Does It Mean To Be A Person of Faith?

With all that is going on in the world today I want to challenge your belief system, or what you believe in, and what it is based upon. "When I say belief system; what is your believing based upon the world system, sensor mechanism, or upon God's system the Word of God, Faith spiritual sensor mechanism?"

Thomas doubts the other apostles' accounts of the Resurrection

According to *John 20:19-29*,

> "[19]Then the same day at evening, being the first day of the week, when the doors were shut where the disciples were assembled for fear of the Jews, came Jesus and stood in the midst, and saith unto them, "Peace be unto you." [20]And when he had so said, he shewed unto them his hands and his side. Then were the disciples glad, when they saw the LORD. [21]Then said Jesus to them again, Peace be unto you: as my Father hath sent me, even so send I you." [22]And when he had said this, he breathed on them, and saith unto them, "Receive ye the Holy Ghost: [23]Whose soever sins ye remit, they are remitted unto them; and whose soever sins ye retain, they are retained." [24]But Thomas, one of the twelve, called Didymus, was not with them when Jesus came. [25]The other disciples therefore said unto him, "we have seen the LORD. But he said unto them," "Except I shall see in his hands the print of the nails, and put my finger into the print of the nails, and thrust my hand into his side, I will not believe." [26]And after eight days, again his disciples were within, and Thomas with them: then came Jesus, the doors being shut, and stood in the midst, and said, Peace be unto you.

> "²⁷Then saith he to Thomas, "Reach hither thy finger, and behold my hands; and reach hither thy hand, and thrust it into my side: and be not faithless, but believing. ²⁸And Thomas answered and said unto him, "My LORD and my God," ²⁹Jesus saith unto him, "Thomas, because thou hast seen me, thou hast believed: blessed are they that have not seen, and yet have believed."

We will be surprise at the number of believers who don't know what they believe. This is because their belief is based upon the wrong system. Yet, they are called believers, but in what do they believe?

When we speak of faith, we are talking about the kind of faith that moves the hand of God! What we're talking about is the faith of the Bible. The kind of faith that Jesus used when he quailed the storm, the kind of faith that Jesus used when he raised the dead, the kind of faith that Jesus used when he ministered to the sick, the kind of faith that Jesus used when he cast out demons.

The scriptures that follow are examples of the kind of faith to which I am referring.

According to *Matthew 9:27-29;*

> "²⁷And when Jesus departed thence, two blind men followed him, crying, and saying, "Thou son of David, have mercy on us." ²⁸And when he was come into the house, the blind men came to him: and Jesus saith unto them, "Believe ye that I am able to do this?" They said unto him, "Yea, Lord." ²⁹Then touched he their eyes, saying, "According to your faith, be it unto you."

Understanding the Working of Faith

In *Matthew 14:22-31* we find;

> "²²And straightway Jesus constrained his disciples to get into a ship, and to go before him unto the other side, while he sent the multitudes away. ²³And when he had sent the multitudes away, he went up into a mountain apart to pray: and when the evening was come, he was there alone. ²⁴But the ship was now in the midst of the sea, tossed with waves, for the wind was contrary. ²⁵And in the fourth watch of the night Jesus went unto them, walking on the sea. ²⁶And when the disciples saw him walking on the sea, they were troubled, saying, "It is a spirit;" and they cried out for fear. ²⁷But straightway Jesus spake unto them, saying, "Be of good cheer; it is I; be not afraid," ²⁸And Peter answered him and said, "Lord, if it be thou, bid me come unto thee on the water. ²⁹And he said, "Come." And when Peter was come down out of the ship, he walked on the water, to go to Jesus. ³⁰But when he saw the wind boisterous, he was afraid; and beginning to sink, he cried, saying, "Lord, save me." ³¹And immediately Jesus stretched forth his hand, and caught him, and said unto him, "O thou of little faith, wherefore didst thou doubt?"

In *Mark 4:36-40* state;

> "³⁶And when they had sent away the multitude, they took him even as he was in the ship. And there were also with him other little ships. ³⁷And there arose a great storm of wind, and the waves beat into the ship, so that it was now full. ³⁸And he was in the hinder part of the ship, asleep on a pillow: and they awake him, and say unto him, "Master, carest thou not that we perish?" ³⁹And he arose, and rebuked the wind, and said unto the sea, "Peace, be still." And the wind ceased, and there was a great calm. ⁴⁰And he said unto them, "Why are ye so fearful? How is it that ye have no faith?"

Understanding the Working of Faith

According to Matthew 15:22-28;

"²²And, behold, a woman of Canaan came out of the same coasts, and cried unto him, saying, "Have mercy on me, O Lord, thou son of David; my daughter is grievously vexed with a devil." ²³But he answered her not a word. And his disciples came and besought him, saying; Send her away; for she crieth after us." ²⁴But he answered and said, "I am not sent but unto the lost sheep of the house of Israel." ²⁵Then came she and worshipped him, saying, "Lord, help me." ²⁶But he answered and said, "It is not meet to take the children's bread, and to cast it to dogs." ²⁷And she said, Truth, Lord: yet the dogs eat of the crumbs which fall from their masters' table." ²⁸Then Jesus answered and said unto her, "O woman, great is thy faith: be it unto thee even as thou wilt." And her daughter was made whole from that very hour."

According to *Mark 5:25-34;*

"²⁵And a certain woman, which had an issue of blood twelve years, ²⁶And had suffered many things of many physicians, and had spent all that she had, and was nothing bettered, but rather grew worse, ²⁷When she had heard of Jesus, came in the press behind, and touched his garment. ²⁸For she said, "If I may touch but his clothes, I shall be whole." ²⁹And straightway the fountain of her blood was dried up; and she felt in her body that she was healed of that plague. ³⁰And Jesus, immediately knowing in himself that virtue had gone out of him, turned him about in the press, and said, "Who touched my clothes? ³¹And his disciples said unto him, "Thou seest the multitude thronging thee, and sayest thou, Who touched me?" ³²And he looked round about to see her that had done this thing. ³³But the woman fearing and trembling, knowing what was done in her, came and fell down before him, and told him all the truth.

[34] And he said unto her, "Daughter, thy faith hath made thee whole; go in peace, and be whole of thy plague."

According to *Luke 7:1-9*;

"[1] Now when he had ended all his sayings in the audience of the people, he entered into Capernaum [2] And a certain centurion's servant, who was dear unto him, was sick, and ready to die. [3] And when he heard of Jesus, he sent unto him the elders of the Jews, beseeching him that he would come and heal his servant. [4] And when they came to Jesus, they besought him instantly, saying, that he was worthy for whom he should do this: [5] For he loveth our nation, and he hath built us a synagogue. [6] Then Jesus went with them. And when he was now not far from the house, the centurion sent friends to him, saying unto him, "Lord, trouble not thyself: for I am not worthy that thou shouldest enter under my roof: [7] Wherefore neither thought I myself worthy to come unto thee: but say in a word, and my servant shall be healed. [8] For I also am a man set under authority, having under me soldiers, and I say unto one, Go, and he goeth; and to another, Come, and he cometh; and to my servant, Do this, and he doeth it." [9] When Jesus heard these things, he marveled at him, and turned him about, and said unto the people that followed him, "I say unto you, I have not found so great faith, no, not in Israel."

Understanding the Working of Faith

According to *Luke 7:36-50;*

"³⁶And one of the Pharisees desired him that he would eat with him and he went into the Pharisee's house, and sat down to meat ³⁷And, behold, a woman in the city, which was a sinner, when she knew that Jesus sat at meat in the Pharisee's house, brought an alabaster box of ointment, ³⁸And stood at his feet behind him weeping, and began to wash his feet with tears, and did wipe them with the hairs of her head, and kissed his feet, and anointed them with the ointment. ³⁹Now when the Pharisee which had bidden him saw it, he spake within himself, saying, "This man, if he were a prophet, would have known who and what manner of woman this is that toucheth him: for she is a sinner. ⁴⁰And Jesus answering said unto him, "Simon, I have somewhat to say unto thee." And he saith, "Master, say on." "⁴¹There was a certain creditor which had two debtors: the one owed five hundred pence, and the other fifty. ⁴²And when they had nothing to pay, he frankly forgave them both. Tell me therefore, which of them will love him most?" ⁴³Simon answered and said, "I suppose that he, to whom he forgave most." And he said unto him, Thou hast rightly judged." ⁴⁴And he turned to the woman, and said unto Simon, "Seest thou this woman? I entered into thine house, thou gavest me no water for my feet: but she hath washed my feet with tears, and wiped them with the hairs of her head. ⁴⁵Thou gavest me no kiss: but this woman since the time I came in hath not ceased to kiss my feet. ⁴⁶My head with oil thou didst not anoint: but this woman hath anointed my feet with ointment. ⁴⁷Wherefore I say unto thee, Her sins, which are many, are forgiven; for she loved much: but to whom little is forgiven, the same loveth little." ⁴⁸And he said unto her, "Thy sins are forgiven."

> ⁴⁹And they that sat at meat with him began to say within themselves, Who is this that forgiveth sins also? ⁵⁰And he said to the woman, "Thy faith hath saved thee; go in peace."

As we share thoughts, ideas, and scriptures on the subject of faith, we know that there are some things that can only acquired through Faith.

1. *Salvation come through Faith*: Ephesians 2:8-9: "⁸For by grace are ye saved through faith; and that not of yourselves: it is the gift of God: ⁹Not of works, lest any man should boast."

2. *The lifestyle of the just is by Faith*: Romans 1:17: "¹⁷For therein is the righteousness of God revealed from faith to faith: as it is written, The just shall live by faith."

3. *The only fight of the believers is of Faith*: 1Timothy 6:12: "¹²Fight the good fight of faith, lay hold on eternal life, whereunto thou art also called, and hast professed a good profession before many witnesses."

4. *The means by which we overcome the world systems is through Faith*: 1 John 5:4: "⁴For whatsoever is born of God overcometh the world: and this is the victory that overcometh the world, even our faith."

5. *The way we please God is thought faith:* Hebrew 11:6: "⁶But without faith it is impossible to please him: for he that cometh to God must believe that he is, and that he is a rewarder of them that diligently seek him."

6. *Two kingdoms on one planted; Duality of existence* this means that things exist in two realms, Spiritual and Natural. They exist first of all in a spiritual realm and second of all in a natural realm.

What we see with our natural eyes is the physical or natural realm. As a driver of a vehicle, when we are about to pull onto the highway and we see a vehicle coming, we are seeing things from a natural perspective, through our physical senses (eyes/sight). The Spiritual realm is where God is; it exists, out there, in God's world.

There are many verses that clearly show the existence of the two realms. Some examples of these verses are listed below.

According to *II Kings 6:12-17*;

> "12And one of his servants said, "None, my lord, O king: but Elisha, the prophet that is in Israel, telleth the king of Israel the words that thou speakest in thy bedchamber" 13And he said, Go and spy where he is, that I may send and fetch him. And it was told him, saying, "Behold, he is in Dothan." 14Therefore sent he thither horses, and chariots, and a great host: and they came by night, and compassed the city about. 15And when the servant of the man of God was risen early, and gone forth, behold, an host compassed the city both with horses and chariots. And his servant said unto him, "Alas, my master! How shall we do?" 16And he answered, "Fear not: for they that be with us are more than they that be with them." 17And Elisha prayed, and said, "LORD, I pray thee, open his eyes, that he may see." "And the LORD opened the eyes of the young man; and he saw: and, behold, the mountain was full of horses and chariots of fire round about Elisha.

According to *2 Corinthians 4:13-15, 18;*

> "¹³We having the same spirit of faith, according as it is written, I believed, and therefore have I spoken; we also believe, and therefore speak; ¹⁴Knowing that he which raised up the Lord Jesus shall raise up us also by Jesus, and shall present us with you. ¹⁵For all things are for your sakes, that the abundant grace might through the thanksgiving of many redound to the glory of God." *2 Corinthians 4:18,* "¹⁸While we look not at the things which are seen, but at the things which are not seen: for the things which are seen are temporal; but the things which are not seen are eternal."

In *Mark 11:22-24* we find;

> "²²And Jesus answering saith unto them, 'Have faith in God. ²³For verily I say unto you, That whosoever shall say unto this mountain, Be thou removed, and be thou cast into the sea; and shall not doubt in his heart, but shall believe that those things which he saith shall come to pass; he shall have whatsoever he saith. ²⁴Therefore I say unto you, what things soever ye desire, when ye pray, believe that ye receive them, and ye shall have them.'

Summary

To be a success, when we are participants in the things of God, it is necessary to know the ground rules, so that we can participate with the Spirit of God and so that we can operate in line with God's word. This can only be done through, and we must understanding, the working of Faith.

Confession

PLEASE READ THIS CONFESSION ALOUD SO THAT THE OUTER EAR CAN HEAR, SO WE CAN BELIEVE SO THAT OUR FAITH WILL INCREASE. AS HUMAN BEINGS, WE PROCESS THINGS AS FOLLOWS: WE THINK IT, WE SAY IT, AND WE DO IT. BUT WITH GOD, WE KNOW THAT FAITH COMETH BY HEARING AND HEARING BY THE WORD OF GOD. WHEN WE FOLLOW THIS PRINCIPLE, WE WILL BE ABLE TO WALK IT OUT.

Jesus is the High Priest of my confession, I hold fast to my confession of faith. I decide to walk by faith and practice faith. My faith comes by hearing and hearing by the Word of God. Jesus is the author and the developer of my faith. I take my shield of faith and quench every fiery dart that the wicked one brings against me. I am a believer and not a doubter. I am the just, I live by faith, and I please my Heavenly Father. I am born of God; I have the victory over the world systems because I am a person of faith.

2. How Do We Get the God kind of Faith?

God is a God of Faith, and it is through the Operation of Faith, that there are over a billion Christians in the world today. Initially, we are given the measure of Faith.

According to *Romans 12:3B* according as God hath dealth to every man the measure of faith;" From this point on we are to increase our faith. We can have little faith or great faith, we can have weak or strong faith. So when we speak of Faith, we are talking about the kind of faith that moves the hand of God, What are talking about is the faith that is referenced in the Bible.

I remember one young man, when I was doing a book signing. He can to my book table and inquired about my faith. Asking what faith did I belong to? I asked, why are you asking me such a question? I knew what he meant, but I acted as if I didn't know what he meant. He said I am a COGI. I asked what is a COGI, as if I didn't know. He said COGI is short for Church of God in Christ. In this book, we are not talking about specific denominations, but we are talking about the faith of God that is based upon the Bible.

So my question is how do we get the Faith that the Bible speaks of?

> Romans 10:17;
>
> "So then faith cometh by hearing, and hearing by the word of God"

Most people want the kind of faith that Jesus used when he quailed the storm; the kind of faith that Jesus used when he raised the dead.

Again, we are talking about the kind of faith that Jesus used when he ministered to the sick; the kind of faith that Jesus used when he casted out demons, in other words the kind of faith that moves the hand of God.

What is Faith? *Hebrews 11:1* tells us,

> "Now faith is the substance of things hoped for, the evidence of things not seen."

In examining this verse we notice that faith is a substance. It has been stated that hope alone is bad or is of no use, but if we add faith to our hope, this is good. It is like a man that has treasure buried on a mountain, but has no way to get a cross to the mountain, so he hopes with faith, because faith is a substance; it can build the bridge that will enable him to access the mountain.

According to *2 Corinthians 5:7;*

> "For we walk by the word and not by the senses"

Did you notice that we have a choice, if we are obedient believers? As a human being, we have a choice to walk by our senses, which is according to the flesh, or according to the word of God, which is according to the Operation of Faith.

According to *John 4:24;*

> "God is a Spirit: and they that worship him must worship him in spirit and in truth."

We see the Operation of Faith when Jesus talks to the woman at Cypress well in Samaria. He tells her that God is a Spirit; therefore He lives in a spirit world. Although the spirit world is not tangible like the physical world, it is, nonetheless, just as real. In fact, as previously stated, it is more realistic that the physical world.

What is more real? The Bible says that in the beginning God created the heavens and the earth, so if God, who is a spirit, created all material things, this means that God would have to have been in existence before he created the material things. Therefore, God must be more real than the things he created, because the things he created depend upon Him; not He upon them.

Again, the Duality of Existence means that things exist in two forms. It exists, first of all, in a spirit form, a form that is outside the realm of our physical senses. This form is the world where God is. The other form is the physical realm; the realm we see. If we think about it while a person is reading and enjoying this good book, there are AM and FM radio waves, being transmitted throughout this immediate area. Just because we can't see them, doesn't mean they don't exist.

At this time let me share with you some biblical examples of the duality of existences that are within the Holy Scriptures.

According to *2 Kings 6:12-17*, as we have seen from Chapter 1, the things that God has for us already exist in the spirit realm, but the way in which they are transferred to the natural realm is through faith.

According to *2 Corinthians 4:18*; as born-again believers, we have been blessed with a measure of Faith.

It states in *Romans 12:3ᴮ* "according as God hath dealt to every man the measure of faith."

How do we Acquire Faith? God provides many scriptures in response to this question.

In *Romans 10:8 -14;*

> "⁸But what saith it? The word is nigh thee, even in thy mouth, and in thy heart: that is, the word of faith, which we preach; ⁹That if thou shalt confess with thy mouth the Lord Jesus, and shalt believe in thine heart that God hath raised him from the dead, thou shalt be saved. ¹⁰For with the heart man believeth unto righteousness; and with the mouth confession is made unto salvation. ¹¹For the scripture saith, whosoever believeth on him shall not be ashamed. ¹²For there is no difference between the Jew and the Greek: for the same Lord over all is rich unto all that call upon him. ¹³For whosoever shall call upon the name of the Lord shall be saved. ¹⁴How then shall they call on him in whom they have not believed? and how shall they believe in him of whom they have not heard? and how shall they hear without a preacher?"

According to *Romans 10:17;*
> "So then faith cometh by hearing, and hearing by the word of God;"

Faith for Salvation:

Ephesians 2:8-9 states;
> "⁸For by grace are ye saved through faith; and that not of yourselves: it is the gift of God: ⁹Not of works, lest any man should boast."

Understanding the Working of Faith

According to *Acts 11:13,14*;

> "¹³And he shewed us how he had seen an angel in his house, which stood and said unto him, Send men to Joppa, and call for Simon, whose surname is Peter; ¹⁴Who shall tell thee words, whereby thou and all thy house shall be saved."

Faith for Prosperity:

3 John 2 states;

> "Beloved, I wish above all things that thou mayest prosper and be in health, even as thy soul prospereth."

Psalm 35:27 tells us;

> "Let them shout for joy, and be glad, that favour my righteous cause: yea, let them say continually, Let the LORD be magnified, which hath pleasure in the prosperity of his servant."

John 10:10 we are told;

> "The thief cometh not, but for to steal, and to kill, and to destroy:"

I am come that they might have life, and that they might have it more abundantly.

Proverbs 13:22 tells us;

> "A good man leaveth an inheritance to his children's children: and the wealth of the sinner is laid up for the just."

Deuteronomy 8:18 states;

> "But thou shalt remember the LORD thy God: for it is he that giveth thee power to get wealth, that he may establish his covenant which he sware unto thy fathers, as it is this day."

Faith for Healing: Let's look at the example found in the book of Acts. We will focus on Paul and what happened when was ministering to a man in Lystra.

According to *Acts 14:7-10*;

> "⁷And there they preached the gospel; ⁸And there sat a certain man at Lystra, impotent in his feet, being a cripple from his mother's womb, who never had walked: ⁹The same heard Paul speak: who steadfastly beholding him, and perceiving that he had faith to be healed, ¹⁰Said with a loud voice, Stand upright on thy feet. And he leaped and walked."

According to *Acts 8:5-8*;

> "⁵Then Philip went down to the city of Samaria, and preached Christ unto them ⁶And the people with one accord gave heed unto those things which Philip spake, hearing and seeing the miracles which he did. ⁷For unclean spirits, crying with loud voice, came out of many that were possessed with them: and many taken with palsies, and that were lame, were healed. ⁸And there was great joy in that city."

Paul did three things:

1. He preached the Gospel (v7)
2. He perceived that the man had faith to be healed (v9)
3. He told the man to stand up and walk v10

The man did three things:

1. Heard Paul preach (v9,)
2. He had faith to be healed (v9)
3. He leaped and walked (v10.)

Summary

How do we get Faith? We have seen from the biblical examples, the God kind of Faith comes only by hearing the Word of God. When we received the Jesus Christ as our Lord and Savior, we were acting in accordance with 2 *Corinthians 4:13,* If we are to be successful in the things of God, it is imperative to know what the ground rules are, so that we can co-labour with the Spirit of God and thus operate in line with God's word.

Confession

PLEASE READ THIS CONFESSION ALOUD SO THAT THE OUTER EAR CAN HEAR, SO WE CAN BELIEVE SO THAT OUR FAITH WILL INCREASE. AS HUMAN BEINGS, WE PROCESS THINGS AS FOLLOWS: WE THINK IT, WE SAY IT, AND WE DO IT. BUT WITH GOD, WE KNOW THAT FAITH COMETH BY HEARING AND HEARING BY THE WORD OF GOD. WHEN WE FOLLOW THIS PRINCIPLE, WE WILL BE ABLE TO WALK IT OUT.

Jesus is the High Priest of my confession, I hold fast to my confession of faith. I decide to walk by faith and practice faith. My faith comes by hearing and hearing by the Word of God. Jesus is the author and the developer of my faith. I take my shield of faith and quench every fiery dart that the wicked one brings against me. I am a believer and not a doubter. I am the just, I live by faith, and I please my Heavenly Father. I am born of God; I have the victory over the world systems because I am a person of faith.

3. Faith, the Operation of God

Faith is acting on the WORD. It is not on your sensory mechanism, some philosophical reasoning, nor on theological concepts, but it's acting on God's Word.

In *Romans 10:9-10 (NTL) says...* "If you confess with your mouth that Jesus is Lord and believe in your heart that God raised him from the dead, you will be saved For it is by believing in your heart that you are made right with God, and it is by confessing with your mouth that you are saved."

In *Romans 3:27* we find, "27Where is boasting then? It is excluded. By what law? of works? Nay: but by the law of faith."

In order to participate in the operation of faith you must have *three* things:
1. You must have the Word of God *(Logos\Rhema)*
2. A Heart that believes the Word of God *(1 Peter 3:4)*
3. A Mouth that speaks (confesses) the Word of God *(Proverb 18:21)*

Some scriptural illustrations are given to show what the Word of God is teaching us - the secret of faith. To be a co-labor with the Spirit of God, it is necessary to know what the ground rules are so that we can operate in faith.

Listed below some examples of the Operations of Faith:
1. God said, "Let there be" *Genesis 17:3-5* "Father of many nations"
2. Conquest of Jericho: *Joshua 6:1-16, 20;* "Walk around the wall"
3. Naaman, the Syria healed: *2 King 5:1-4, 8 -14;* "Dip seven times"
4. Peter acting on the Word of God: *Luke 5:1-9; (v5)* "let down the net"

Understanding the Working of Faith

The simplest way to the operation of faith, is learn to believe the Word to the point that you will act on it. You don't know if you are really a believer until you are willing to demonstrate your belief. It is through acting on the Word of God that you move from believing to faith. *James 1:22* states that, "We are not to be hearers only, but doers of the Word of God."

The operation of faith calls those things, which be not as though they were. Instead of them being based upon what you see; they are based upon the Word of God.

The universe, in which live, contain many laws. One that we are very familiar with is the law of gravity. Everyone knows what goes up must come down.

The law, by which we access the things of God, is called the Law of Faith.

The Law of Faith, operates when we learn to, "Call those things which be not as though they were", according to *2 Corinthians 4:18*. We can apply this law, because we are born-again.

There are many who operate in faith from a negative prospective. Listed below are some examples of negative phrases that people use without realizing it.

1. "My feet are killing me." (1 Peter 2:24)
2. "I am scared to death." (2 Timothy 1:7)
3. "I am confused." (1 Corinthians 14:30)
4. "I am broke, busted, and can't be trusted" (Phil. 4:19)
5. "Well if it's not one things it is another" (Mark 11:23)
6. "I am so weak" (Joel 3:10b)
7. "Girl I am about to lose my mind" (1Corinthians. 2:16)

We, as believers, have the ability of operate in faith without an understanding the workings of faith. It is the enemy who is influencing us to use such phrases because he knows that it is detrimental to our lives. By understanding the proper working of faith, we can receive the wonderful blessings of God.

"Therefore being justified by faith, we have peace with God through Our Lord Jesus Christ: By whom also we have access by faith into this grace wherein we stand, and rejoice in hope of the glory of God and not only so, but we glory in tribulations also: knowing that tribulation worketh patience;"   (Romans 5:1-3)

As believers, we have the God kind of faith and must act according to Mark 11:22-24;

> "And Jesus answering saith unto them, Have faith in God. [23]For verily I say unto you, That whosoever shall say unto this mountain, Be thou removed, and be thou cast into the sea; and shall not doubt in his heart, but shall believe that those things which he saith shall come to pass; he shall have whatsoever he saith. [24]Therefore I say unto you, what things soever ye desire, when ye pray, believe that ye receive them, and ye shall have them."

I trust that you have seen from the biblical examples how the operations of the God kind of faith, works. In order to be successful in the things of God, it is necessary to know what the ground rules are, so that we can be co-laborers with the Spirit of God. It is through faith that we have access to the wonderful blessings that He has for us to enjoy while on earth.

Summary

Faith is trusting in God and not man. For man has the ability to fail, whereas, God never fails. When you walk by faith, there is no room for doubts. When you walk by faith, there is no time for worries. When you walk by faith, mountains will be moved. Always know God's word, have a believing heart and confess with your mouth God's word. According to Hebrews 11:6, it states that without faith it is impossible to please God,

Confession

PLEASE READ THIS CONFESSION ALOUD SO THAT THE OUTER EAR CAN HEAR, SO WE CAN BELIEVE SO THAT OUR FAITH WILL INCREASE. AS HUMAN BEINGS, AND WE PROCESS THINGS AS FOLLOWS: WE THINK IT, WE SAY IT, AND WE DO IT. BUT WITH GOD, WE KNOW THAT FAITH COMETH BY HEARING AND HEARING BY THE WORD OF GOD. WHEN WE FOLLOW THIS PRINCIPLE, WE WILL BE ABLE TO WALK IT OUT.

Jesus is the High Priest of my confession, I hold fast to my confession of faith. I decide to walk by faith and practice faith. My faith comes by hearing and hearing by the Word of God. Jesus is the author and the developer of my faith. I take my shield of faith and quench every fiery dart that the wicked one brings against me. I am a believer and not a doubter. I am the just, I live by faith, and I please my Heavenly Father. I am born of God; I have the victory over the world systems because I am a person of faith.

4. Activating the Power of God through faith

When we truly understand the working of Faith, it is God who gives us authority in the earth as his representative, and it is when we exercise our God given authority, God will activate His ability (POWER).

According to *Isaiah 55:11;*

> "So shall my word be that goeth forth out of my mouth: it shall not return unto me void, but it shall accomplish that which I please, and it shall prosper in the thing whereto I sent it."

According to *Jeremiah 1:12;*

> "Then said the LORD unto me, Thou hast well seen: for I will hasten my word to perform it."

When we talk about the Operation of Faith, most of us understand what is happening from a natural perspective. But in this book, I want to go behind the scenes, and show you the working of faith from a spiritual perspective; in the spirit realm. We have to understand that we are living in a physical, material, three dimensional world that can be contacted with our physical senses. However, at the center and core of our being, we are a spirit. We do not have a spirit, we are one! We have a soul, and we live inside a physical body.

With our spirit, we contact the realm of God who is a Spirit. With our body, through our five senses, we contact the physical and material universe around us. And with our soul, which contains our desires, our will, our emotions and our intellect, we contact the emotional and intellectual realm. Man-kind can operate in three different worlds at the same time.

When Hollywood comes out with a new movie, it shows us the parts that they want us to see, and that is the movie itself. Eventually, the movie comes out on DVD, and the DVD will have extra scenes, where they show us how different stunts are done, when making the movie. Again, I want to show you what happens in the spirit realm, when we, as believers of the Word of God, believe with our hearts and speak it in Faith.

As previously shared in *Isaiah 55: 8-11* and *Jeremiah 1:12*, God says I watch over my word to perform it In order to better understand this statement, we must know the present day minister is our Lord and Savior Jesus, who is the Christ, And according to Hebrews 4:14, "Jesus is our High Priest, and it states that we are to hold fast to our profession, but in the literal Greek the word profession is the word confession."

In *Hebrews 10:23*, again, we are told again to hold fast to our profession, and again in the literal Greek the word profession is the word confession. If we truly understand what is be said here it means to hold fast to our confession. It means that we are to hold fast to the promises that are found in the Word of God.

As we literally speak or confess the Word of God, which is the promise of God, according to *Hebrews 1:14*, the angels of God are ministering spirits sent to minister on the behalf of the saints or believers who have received the Lord Jesus Christ as their Lord and Savior.

In *Psalm 103:20-21*, it states that the angels excel in strength, and they listen to us, as believers, and when we speak or confess the Word of God or the promises of God, they see to it that a connection is made with our High Priest, that the Word of God or promises of God are manifested in our lives.

Another classic example of activating the power of God and the raising of her son from the dead is found in the Old Testament.

According to *2 Kings 4: 8-37*, we have the story of the Shunammite women that was blessed with a son. When the son was grown and working in the field with his father, he became sick with a headache. The father told his son to go and sit on the porch with his mother, and while sitting with his mother on the porch, the son died.

Please note the reaction of the mother. The mother took her son and laid him on the bed of the man of God. Then she called out to her husband and asked him to send her a young man and one of the donkeys, so that she may go to the man of God. Her husband asked what was wrong, and her response in verse 23 was, "it shall be well." (Please note the mother's response).

When the man of God saw the Shunammite afar, He sent his servant to see if everything was alright? So Ghehazi ran unto the Shunammite women and asked if ever thing was ok with her family. According *2 Kings 4:26*, her reply was, "*It is well*" (Please note her response) and according to *2 Kings 4:35-37*, her son was raise from the dead and presented to his mother. At no time during this ordeal did she state that her son was dead.

The Shunammite woman's reply was, "It shall be well" and "it is well". She never spoke the problem, she only spoke the answer.

In reflecting back on *Isaiah 55:8-11* and *Jeremiah 1:12* (God says, "I watch over my word to perform it". When we, as believers, speak God's word, we are activating the power of God on our behalf. As we note the response of the Shunammite women, it was never the problem but only the answer. Another classic example of activating the power of God is in the New Testament: Zacharias and the birth of John the Baptist John *Luke 1:5-20*, we have the angel Gabriel being sent from the presence of God to Zacharias, sharing with him about the birth of John Baptist. Zacharias was made unable to speak until the plan of God was fulfilled, because of the power of (HIS) words.

According to *Luke 1:20*, "And, behold, thou shalt be dumb, and not able to speak, until the day that these things shall be performed, because thou believest not my words, which shall be fulfilled in their season"

According to *Mark 5:25-34*; Woman with an issue of blood active the power of God and received her healing when she touched His clothes in faith, thus activating the power of God to receive her healing.

Summary

Many believers' think that when we speak words, we are just making noise, but words are spirit, and they can either help or hinder the plan of God. *2 Corinthians 4:18* tells us, we must learn to cooperate with the Spirit of God by knowing the power of our words, and it is through words of faith that we can access the things of God.

Confession

PLEASE READ THIS CONFESSION ALOUD SO THAT THE OUTER EAR CAN HEAR, SO WE CAN BELIEVE SO THAT OUR FAITH WILL INCREASE. AS HUMAN BEINGS, AND WE PROCESS THINGS AS FOLLOWS: WE THINK IT, WE SAY IT, AND WE DO IT. BUT WITH GOD, WE KNOW THAT FAITH COMETH BY HEARING AND HEARING BY THE WORD OF GOD. WHEN WE FOLLOW THIS PRINCIPLE, WE WILL BE ABLE TO WALK IT OUT.

Jesus is the High Priest of my confession, I hold fast to my confession of faith. I decide to walk by faith and practice faith. My faith comes by hearing and hearing by the Word of God. Jesus is the author and the developer of my faith. I take my shield of faith and quench every fiery dart that the wicked one brings against me. I am a believer and not a doubter. I am the just, I live by faith, and I please my Heavenly Father. I am born of God; I have the victory over the world systems because I am a person of faith.

5. Faith and Belief are not the same

There are two words used throughout the scriptures which are always used separately and independently. Yet in the natural or in everyday life, we tend to make these two words synonymous terms. They are different words - spelled differently, pronounced differently - yet we make both words mean the same thing in our lives and in our actions. The words are: faith and belief. Most people think faith and belief are the same. Most people think believing is faith, or faith is believing.

In *Mark 9:23* we find the following,

> "Jesus said unto him, "If thou canst believe, all things are possible to him that believeth"

The Word of God says in *Romans 10:9-10;*

> "That if thou shalt confess with thy mouth the Lord Jesus, and shalt believe in thine heart that God hath raised him from the dead, thou shalt be saved. [10]For with the heart man believeth unto righteousness; and with the mouth confession is made unto salvation."

Some people think, "If I believe, that's faith," and "If I have faith, it means I believe." Belief or believe means to have a total commitment to God, it means that you are sold out to the word of God, and you don't have a backup plan.

First example: In my life, I remember a time when I was preparing to attend Bible College. I was living in New Jersey and the school I was planning to attend was in Tulsa, Oklahoma. April of 1981, I made a list of what I needed in order to attend school in Oklahoma.

Understanding the Working of Faith

The list is as follows:

1. I had a car that I needed to be transport to Tulsa Ok
2. I needed a truck to take my personal belongings.
3. I had a house that needed to be rented.
4. I had a family that I needed to relocate.
5. I needed a job to support my family.
6. I needed a house for my family.
7. I needed some money.

Once I completed my list of what was needed in order to move to Oklahoma by April of 1981, I PRAYED THE PRAY OF FAITH for everything that I needed on that list. I lived near a park that was about a mile in length and each day after work, I walked around that park giving thanks to God that I believe that I receive everything on my list, and counted it as done by Faith. I did this every day until I left at the end of August of 1981, (approximately one hundred and forty days). Around the second week in August my friend Timothy, who was already in Tulsa, Oklahoma, was coming to New Jersey for a wedding. I was able to contact him, and he was able to drive my car back to Tulsa Oklahoma. Number 1, getting the car transported to Oklahoma was removed from my list.

I received my last pay check at the end of August. After paying my last few bills I had only $300.00 left. Therefore, I had enough money to rent a Ryder truck. I gathered up my family (wife and two sons). Number 2, needing a truck to load and carry personal belongings was removed from my list!

I remember saying to God, "If I end up in Timbuktu, it is on you, because I believe that I am doing what you want me to do." Remember, I still had my list of things that I believed that I receive everything on my list, and I had counted it as done by faith. In the natural, our house had not been rented and we did not know where we were going to stay once we got to Oklahoma. I did not have a job lined up, and I only had a $300.00 in my pocket. I remember heading south. Just before we got on New Jersey Turnpike, I call my pastor, Clinton Utterrback, of Redeeming Love Christian Center, to tell him that we were on our way. Just in case you don't understand, I believe I heard from God, and I took Him at His word with no backup plan.

As we travelled to Oklahoma, and stopped to fill up the Ryder truck, it cost $50.00 each time. I remember I was down to my last $50.00 somewhere in Pennsylvania. After filling up the truck, I went in and paid for the gas. When I got to the truck, and started to get back in, I saw an envelope. I picked it up and got into the truck.

I looked in the envelope and it contained all one hundred dollar bills ($2,500.00). As cool as I am, I stayed focused and continued on my way to Oklahoma. As we continued on our way, I was just Praising God for the financial blessing. I was thinking that somewhere along the line, somebody would give me some money. After all, I was a Christian, I had a lot of Christian friends, and they knew I was relocating my family to Oklahoma so I could attend school.

I thought, maybe the church, or some of my friends would give me something, but no one did. Number 7, needing money, was removed from my list!

What I did was act upon the Words that God *had given me*, and for the first time, I saw firsthand that God watched over His word and performed it in my life. As I checked my list, I checked off numbers 1, 2, and 7. My house still had not been rented, I still didn't have a job, nor did I know where my family and I were going to stay.

Once we got to Oklahoma we checked into a hotel, and within that first week I met a fellow student by the name of Kevin. Kevin and his family lived in a large house that had a studio apartment with a kitchen, fireplace, and 1 1/2 bathroom. My family and I moved in and lived there for a while. Number 4, relocating my family was removed from my list! Eventually, we got the whole house, and were able to rent out the studio apartment. Number 6, needing a house for my family was removed from my list!

Within that same week, I got a job at the PepsiCo Bottling Company as a computer operator. I worked there the entire time that I was in Oklahoma and continued to work there even after finishing school. Number 5, needing a job to support family was removed from my list!

By the end of September, our house in New Jersey had been rented. The same tenants lived in our house the entire time we were in Oklahoma. Number 3, renting our house was removed from my list! I want you to know that God is faithful to His word, and as a child of God all we have to do is take Him at His word and act on it. The Word of God works if you work it.

All we have to do is take Him at His word and act on it. Remember, I took God at His word and acted on it with no backup plan. God knows when you really trust Him and take Him at His word, and when you don't have a backup plan. Again, to truly believe means that you are making a commitment. As for me, no matter what, I am sticking with the word of God, just like the three Hebrews boys in the book of Daniel.

Another thing I have come to realize is that that most Christians don't really believe, but they give mental accent, (meaning they agree that the Bible is true) but it is different when you believe. When you really believe, you will act on it.

Faith and belief are two sides to the same coin. In the natural, in our economy, we have coins nickels, dimes, quarters, half dollars, and silver dollars. These coins have two sides. One is referred to as the head's side. (It usually has the head of a person, a President, etc., on it.) Its common usage heads and tails.

Understanding the Working of Faith

In our natural economy, in order to use a coin as legal tender, as an instrument of barter in purchasing goods and services, both sides of that coin must be intact. Allow me show you, clearly, the difference between faith and belief, because if you don't know the difference, you will never be able to truly exercise faith.

Please note the examples of faith in the stories that follow.

A man dying of starvation - A man staggers through the door and falls onto the floor. The doctor does a preliminary examination of the man for about 30 minutes. The man died with food in view. Why? He died because he didn't eat the food. The eating of the food is faith! Faith is acting on what you believe.

Woman with an issue of blood – *Mark 5:25-34*, talks about the woman who had an issue of blood for twelve years. She hears about Jesus, and she said if I may touch His clothes I shall be whole. In verse 34 that is exactly what happened.

Man born blind – According to John 9:6, Jesus anointed the eyes of a man born blind and told him to go and wash in the pool Siloam. In verse 7, he went his way therefore, and washed and came seeing.

Faith is ...... acting on what you believe, and you don't believe with your head you believe with your heart. If you don't act on what you believe, you will die just like the man in our illustration, who died of starvation. That is why thousands of Christians, who are prayed for as they lie in hospitals, lovely Christian, who love the Lord, whose names are written in the Lamb's Book of Life, who speak in tongues "die" because of their lack of faith.

Thank God they died and went to heaven. But they died on that bed believing that God could heal them, just as that man believed if he ate the food it would keep him from starving to death. But he still died.

Summary

What you believe may be true. Just as what the man believe was true. We couldn't help his believing. But it didn't help him, did it? He died. Why did he die? Because he did not act on what he believed. He had to eat food before it could do him any personal good. And this action, the eating, is on what we build our faith.

Confession

PLEASE READ THIS CONFESSION ALOUD SO THAT THE OUTER EAR CAN HEAR, SO WE CAN BELIEVE SO THAT OUR FAITH WILL INCREASE. AS HUMAN BEINGS, WE PROCESS THINGS AS FOLLOWS: WE THINK IT, WE SAY IT, AND WE DO IT. BUT WITH GOD, WE KNOW THAT FAITH COMETH BY HEARING AND HEARING BY THE WORD OF GOD. WHEN WE FOLLOW THIS PRINCIPLE, WE WILL BE ABLE TO WALK IT OUT.

Jesus is the High Priest of my confession, I hold fast to my confession of faith. I decide to walk by faith and practice faith. My faith comes by hearing and hearing by the Word of God. Jesus is the author and the developer of my faith. I take my shield of faith and quench every fiery dart that the wicked one brings against me. I am a believer and not a doubter. I am the just, I live by faith, and I please my Heavenly Father. I am born of God; I have the victory over the world systems because I am a person of faith.

6. The Enemies of Faith

In any fight, one must recognize his enemy in order to successfully win a battle. In the believer's case, the devil is the enemy who desires to swindle us out of our rights and privileges in Christ Jesus.

According to 2 Corinthians 2:11;

> "11Lest satan should get an advantage of us: for we are not ignorant of his devices."

According to 1Timothy 6:12;

> "12Fight the good fight of faith, lay hold on eternal life, whereunto thou art also called, and hast professed a good profession before many witnesses."

Enemies Faith:

Have you ever wondered why we don't see more evidence of faith? The Bible identifies several tendencies that undermine faith.

1. **Worry** - Jesus cautioned: ". . . Do not worry . . . But seek first the kingdom of God"

According to *Matthew 6:25-33*;

> "25 Therefore I say unto you, Take no thought for your life, what ye shall eat, or what ye shall drink; nor yet for your body, what ye shall put on. Is not the life more than meat, and the body than raiment? 26 Behold the fowls of the air: for they sow not, neither do they reap, nor gather into barns; yet your heavenly Father feedeth them. Are ye not much better than they? 27 Which of you by taking thought can add one cubit unto his stature? 28 And why take ye thought for raiment? Consider the lilies of the field, how they grow; they toil not, neither do they spin:

Understanding the Working of Faith

> ^{29}And yet I say unto you, That even Solomon in all his glory was not arrayed like one of these. ^{30} Wherefore, if God so clothe the grass of the field, which today is, and tomorrow is cast into the oven, *shall he* not much more *clothe* you, O ye of little faith? ^{31} Therefore take no thought, saying, What shall we eat? or, What shall we drink? or, Wherewithal shall we be clothed? ^{32} (For after all these things do the Gentiles seek:) for your heavenly Father knoweth that ye have need of all these things. ^{33} But seek ye first the kingdom of God, and his righteousness; and all these things shall be added unto you.

In Philippians 4:6, it states;

> "⁶Be careful for nothing; but in everything by prayer and supplication with thanksgiving let your requests be made known unto God."

2. Fear - While on a boat in the middle of a storm, the disciples awoke Jesus and pleaded that He save them from drowning. He answered, "Why are you fearful, O you of little faith?"

Then He rebuked the sea and it immediately grew calm according to *Matthew 8:23-26,*

> "²³And when he was entered into a ship, his disciples followed him. ²⁴And, behold, there arose a great tempest in the sea, insomuch that the ship was covered with the waves: but he was asleep. ²⁵And his disciples came to him, and awoke him, saying, Lord, save us: we perish. ²⁶And he saith unto them, Why are ye fearful, O ye of little faith? Then he arose, and rebuked the winds and the sea; and there was a great calm,"

According to 2 Timothy 1:7;

> "7For God hath not given us the spirit of fear; but of power, and of love, and of a sound mind."

3. Doubt - Peter saw Jesus walking on the water of the Sea of Galilee and asked if he could do the same. Jesus invited him to join Him, and Peter, too, began walking on the water. "But when he saw that the wind was boisterous, he was afraid" and began to sink (*Matthew 14:30*). Christ "stretched out His hand and caught him, and said to him, 'O you of little faith, why did you doubt?' "

4. Human reasoning without Spiritual understanding - Jesus warned His disciples,

Matthew 16:7-12;

> "Take heed and beware of the leaven of the Pharisees and the Sadducees"

He was cautioning them against the teachings of religious leaders who appeared outwardly correct (verse 12) but lacked spiritual understanding. Because the disciples did not understand this spiritual principle, their reasoning was to no avail (verses 7-12).

5. Complaining - Human reasoning without spiritual understanding. Who does not like to grudge, grouch, complain, and criticize? Who hasn't done this? Almost everyone living in every nook and corner of this world does this. And yes, we all are aware of the fact that it's not good to complain or criticize unnecessarily; still we tend to do so.

We must be careful with whom we keep company. If they are people who complain, we can be influence by them. In understanding this from a spiritual perspective, this is a tool of satan to separate us from our faith especially if we join in with them and start complaining.

I remember one time I was watching the Israelites, who were traveling in a movie. As they were on their way to this particular place, they were all saying, "O give thanks unto the Lord, for His mercy endureth forever." As you can see, it is so easy for the flesh to join right in, but we must stay focus.

I have learned to apply this to my life. When I am about to say something negative I've trained myself to say "O give thanks unto the Lord, for His mercy endureth forever." In repeating this statement, I am being a doer of the Word of God and by not allowing any corrupt communication come out of my mouth.

By "doing this", I am not giving place for Satan to use my mouth. By not complaining, satan will not be able to use my complaints as a tool to separate me from my faith.

Summary

Believers must understand how to operate by faith. To operate by faith does not make sense to the natural man. When Christians rely on sense knowledge only, they are robbed of revelation knowledge from God.

Confession

PLEASE READ THIS CONFESSION ALOUD SO THAT THE OUTER EAR CAN HEAR, SO WE CAN BELIEVE SO THAT OUR FAITH WILL INCREASE. AS HUMAN BEINGS, WE PROCESS THINGS AS FOLLOWS: WE THINK IT, WE SAY IT, AND WE DO IT. BUT WITH GOD, WE KNOW THAT FAITH COMETH BY HEARING AND HEARING BY THE WORD OF GOD. WHEN WE FOLLOW THIS PRINCIPLE, WE WILL BE ABLE TO WALK IT OUT.

Jesus is the High Priest of my confession, I hold fast to my confession of faith. I decide to walk by faith and practice faith. My faith comes by hearing and hearing by the Word of God. Jesus is the author and the developer of my faith. I take my shield of faith and quench every fiery dart that the wicked one brings against me. I am a believer and not a doubter. I am the just, I live by faith, and I please my Heavenly Father. I am born of God; I have the victory over the world systems because I am a person of faith.

7. The Law of Faith

Faith is the law of God and it pleases God when we abide by that law. Faith is based upon the word of God and not what can be seen with the human eye. Operating in the law of faith requires us to know the word of God, a heart that believes in God's word, and a mouth that speaks God's word.

According to the Webster's dictionary, the meaning of the word law is, a principle based on the predictable consequences of an act, condition, etc.

Example of other laws:

The law of Faith is like God's law of gravity. It works. Believe it or not, it still works. The law of gravity works all the time. God's law of faith works all the time, as it's God's Law of Attraction! Electricity has laws, and there are also laws of aerodynamics. If you operate within the laws of electricity or aero dynamics, it is safe, performs well and is dependable. However if you break these laws, they can kill you. Likewise, if you operate within the law of faith, it too, will be safe, it will perform for you, and it will be something to depend on.

The problem is that some people don't "work it." The law of gravity is mandatory. The law of faith is optional. But God tells us how to operate in faith. It will work whenever it is applied properly. Faith will not work if we fail to apply it according to God's specified way.

Faith is a law in the sense that electricity has laws, and there are also laws of aerodynamics. If you operate within the laws of electricity or aerodynamics, it is safe, performs well and is dependable. However if you break those laws, it can kill you. Likewise, if you operate within the law of faith, it too, will be safe, perform for you, and will be something to depend on.

In *Romans 3:23-27*;

> "For all have sinned, and come short of the glory of God, 24: Being justified freely by His grace through the redemption that is in Christ Jesus: 25: Whom God hath set forth to be a propitiation through faith in His blood, to declare His righteousness for the remission of sins that are past, through the forbearance of God 26: To declare I say, at this time His righteousness: that he might be just, and the justifier of him which believeth in Jesus, 27: Where is boasting then? It is excluded, by what law? of works? Nay: but by the <u>law of faith</u>.

All of mankind has faith

For l say, through the grace given unto me, to every man that is among you, not to think of himself more highly than he ought to think; but to think soberly, according as God hath dealt to every man the measure of faith. (See *Romans 12:3*) Mankind has a free will to place it in, and exercise it on, whatever he wants. In fact, man is a creature of faith. That is to say that he was created to live by faith.

Man is driven by something in him to place his faith, (like an anchor), in something or someone in the desire to feel safe, sound and whole.

It really becomes a matter of just what his faith is in, as to what result will come of it. For example his faith may be in his education, his money, his strength, his doctor, his lawyer, his preacher, and on and on.

Faith is the Law of God

Hebrews 11:1;

> "Faith is the substance of things hoped for and the evidence of things not seen",

We please God when we operate in Faith.

Hebrews 11:6

> "And without faith it is impossible to please Him, for he who comes to God must believe that He is, and that He is a rewarder of those who seek Him."

We believe that the carnal mind cannot operate in God's Law of Faith.

Romans 3:27;

> "Where is boasting then? It is excluded, by are What law? of works? Nay: but by the law of faith." There other laws like this, for instance, the law of the Spirit of life and the law of sin and death"

Romans 8:1-2;

> "There is therefore now no condemnation to them which are in Christ Jesus, who walk not after the flesh, but after the Spirit, 2: For the law of the Spirit of life in Christ Jesus hath made me free from the law of sin and death."

Romans 12:3;

> "For I say, through the grace given unto me, to every man that is among you, not to think of himself more highly than he ought to think; but to think soberly, according as God hath dealt to every man the measure of faith."

James 1:5-7;

> "⁵If any of you lack wisdom, let him ask of God, that giveth to all men liberally, and upbraideth not; and it shall be given him. ⁶But let him ask in faith, nothing wavering. For he that wavereth is like a wave of the sea driven with the wind and tossed. ⁷For let not that man think that he shall receive any thing of the Lord."

It also states in James that we have to be doers of the Word of God....not just hearers. We have to put our faith to work. Speak it, believe it without doubt!

We find the following in the book of James says …

James 1:23-24;

> "²³For if any be a hearer of the word, and not a doer, he is like unto a man beholding his natural face in a glass: ²⁴For he beholdeth himself, and goeth his way, and straightway forgetteth what manner of man he was."

Faith Obeys the Word! - You have heard the adage "seeing is believing" well, that's not really true.

2 Corinthians 4:18, "

> The Bible indicates that "Believing is seeing through the eyes of Faith"

Understanding the Working of Faith

True Faith is never blind. Faith always knows. Faith always sees. Faith is able to look through the storm and see the end results. Faith will always talk the end results, instead of what exists at present. Faith is acting of the Word of God!

The key to Understanding the Workings of Faith:

Mark 11:22-24;

> "But shall BELIEVE that those things which he SAYS shall come to pass; he shall have whatsoever, (Anything in line with the Word of God), he SAYS In verse twenty four;" therefore I say unto you, what things so-ever ye desire, when ye pray, believe that ye receive them, (Prior to their manifestation), and ye shall have them. (Emphasis added)"

You have to SPEAK His Words concerning healing. You are SPEAKING them to:
1. Confess (affirm) to God
2. Proclaim to the devil and
3. Confirm to yourself that you BELIEVE what you are saying.

The Word of God tells us, "Even so faith, if it hath not works, is dead, being alone." In *James 2:17*;

You must ACT on your faith for it to be released and produce anything! The withered hand had to be stretched out before it was made whole.

In *Matthew 12:9-13*; the Word of God says…

> "⁹And when he was departed thence, he went into their synagogue: ¹⁰And, behold, there was a man which had his hand withered. And they asked him, saying, Is it lawful to heal on the Sabbath days? that they might accuse him, ¹¹And he said unto them, What man shall there be among you, that shall have one sheep, and if it fall into a pit on the sabbath day, will he not lay hold on it, and lift it out? ¹²How much then is a man better than a sheep? Wherefore it is lawful to do well on the Sabbath days. ¹³Then saith he to the man, Stretch forth thine hand. And he stretched it forth; and it was restored whole, like as the other."

We need to DO something that we could not previously do. Our faith has to be based on the written Word of God, whether it is for healing or anything else!

Faith, the Operation of God

Faith is acting on the WORD. It is not on your sensory mechanism, some philosophical reasoning, nor on theological concepts, but it's acting on God's Word.

Romans 10:9-10 NTL;

> "If you confess with your mouth that Jesus is Lord and believe in your heart that God raised him from the dead, you will be saved. For it is by believing in your heart that you are made right with God, and it is by confessing with your mouth that you are saved."

Romans 3:27;

> "²⁷Where is boasting then? It is excluded By what law? of works? Nay: but by the law of faith."

Understanding the Working of Faith

In order to participate in the operation of faith you must have three things:

1. You must have the Word of God *(Logos \ Rhema)*
2. A Heart that believes the Word of God *(1 Peter 3:4)*
3. A Mouth that speaks the Word of God *(Proverb 18:21)*

Some scriptures are given to show what the Word of God is teaching us the secret of faith is to be a co-labor with the Spirit of God, it is necessary to know what the ground rules are so that we can operate in faith.

Listed below some examples of the Operations of Faith:
1. God said, "Let there be" *Genesis 1:3-25;*
2. Abraham "Father of many nations" *Genesis 17:3-40*
3. Conquest of Jericho: *Joshua 6:16 -20;*
4. Naaman, the Syria healed: *2 King 5:1-4, 8-14;*
5. Peter acting on the Word of God. *Luke 5:1-9;*

The simplest way to the operation of faith is to learn to believe the Word and act on it. You don't know if you are really a believer until you are willing to demonstrate your belief. It is through acting on the Word of God that you move from believing to faith. James chapter one and verse twenty two; states that, "We are not to be hearers only, but doers of the Word of God."

The operation of faith calls those things, which be not as though they were. Instead of them being based upon what you see; they are based upon the Word of God. The universe, in which live, contains many laws. Again everyone is very familiar with is the law of gravity. Everyone knows what goes up must come down.

Understanding the Working of Faith

The law, by which we access the things of God, is called the Law of Faith. The Law of Faith operates when we learn to "Call those things which be not as though they were", (*2 Corinthians 4:18*).

We can apply this law, because we are born-again.

"We having the same spirit of faith, according as it is written, I believed, and therefore have I spoken; we also believe, and therefore speak" (*2 Corinthians 4:13*)

There are many who operate in faith from a negative prospective. Listed below are some examples of negative phrases that people use without realizing it.

1. "My feet are killing me." (*1 Peter 2:24*)
2. "I am scared to death." (*2 Timothy 1:7*)
3. "I am confused." (*1 Corinthians 14:30*)
4. "I am broke, busted, can't be trusted"(*Philippians 4:19*)

We, as believers, have the ability of operate in faith without an understanding the workings of faith. It is the enemy who is influencing us to use such phrases because he knows that it is detrimental to our lives.

By understanding the proper working of faith, we can receive the wonderful blessings of God.

Romans 5:1-3;

> "Therefore being justified by faith, we have peace with God through Our Lord Jesus Christ: By whom also we have access by faith into this grace wherein we stand, and rejoice in hope of the glory of God and not only so, but we glory in tribulations also: knowing that tribulation worketh patience;"

As believers, we have the God kind of faith and must act according to *Mark 11:22-24*;

> "²²And Jesus answering saith unto them, Have faith in God. ²³For verily I say unto you, That whosoever shall say unto this mountain, Be thou removed, and be thou cast into the sea; and shall not doubt in his heart, but shall believe that those things which he saith shall come to pass; he shall have whatsoever he saith. ²⁴Therefore I say unto you, what things soever ye desire, when ye pray, believe that ye receive them, and ye shall have them."

I trust that you have seen from the biblical examples how the operations of the God kind of faith, works. In order to be successful in the things of God, it is necessary to know what the ground rules are, so that we can be co-laborers with the Spirit of God. It is through faith that we have access to the wonderful blessings that He has for us to enjoy while on earth.

Summary

Faith is trusting in God and not man. For man has the ability to fail, whereas, God never fails. When you walk by faith, there is no room for doubts. When you walk by faith, there is no time for worries. When you walk by faith, mountains will be moved. Always know God's word, have a believing heart and confess with your mouth God's word.

Confession

PLEASE READ THIS CONFESSION ALOUD SO THAT THE OUTER EAR CAN HEAR, SO WE CAN BELIEVE SO THAT OUR FAITH WILL INCREASE. AS HUMAN BEINGS, WE PROCESS THINGS AS FOLLOWS: WE THINK IT, WE SAY IT, AND WE DO IT. BUT WITH GOD, WE KNOW THAT FAITH COMETH BY HEARING AND HEARING BY THE WORD OF GOD. WHEN WE FOLLOW THIS PRINCIPLE, WE WILL BE ABLE TO WALK IT OUT.

Jesus is the High Priest of my confession, I hold fast to my confession of faith. I decide to walk by faith and practice faith. My faith comes by hearing and hearing by the Word of God. Jesus is the author and the developer of my faith. I take my shield of faith and quench every fiery dart that the wicked one brings against me. I am a believer and not a doubter. I am the just, I live by faith, and I please my Heavenly Father. I am born of God; I have the victory over the world systems because I am a person of faith.

8. Faith is your Servant
Part 1

A servant is a person who serves others, an individual who performs duties for his master whether it be a personal or public matter. When I ask people about what are their thoughts about a servant? Most people, in general, are so servant minded that when I ask the question where is your maid? Their response is I don't need a maid to clean my house. I'll clean my own house. As we have become a Christian, a child of God, we have been blessed with a servant and many Christians are not aware of it.

When we speak of a servant, we are not talking about someone who you can order around to do this and that God has blessed us with a servant who operates strictly in line with His word. When we truly understand the goodness that our Heavenly Father has bestowed upon us as servants, and with His help, we should be victorious in every area of our life.

There are several verses we wish to share with you pertaining to this Servant we call Faith,

Romans 1:16-17;

> "¹⁶For I am not ashamed of the gospel of Christ: for it is the power of God unto salvation to everyone that believeth; to the Jew first, and also to the Greek. ¹⁷For therein is the righteousness of God revealed from faith to faith: as it is written, the just shall live by faith."

Understanding the Working of Faith

Hebrews 10:35-37;

> "Cast not away therefore your confidence, which hath great recompense of reward. ³⁶For ye have need of patience, that, after ye have done the Will of God, ye might receive the promise. ³⁷For yet a little while, and he that shall come will come, and will not tarry. <u>Now the just shall live by faith</u>: but if any man drawback, my soul shall have no pleasure in him."

Habakkuk 2:2-4;

> "²And the LORD answered me, and said, write the vision, and make it plain upon tables, that he may run that readeth it. ³For the vision is yet for an appointed time, but at the end it shall speak, and not lie: though it tarry, wait for it; because it will surely come, it will not tarry. ⁴Behold, his soul which is lifted up is not upright in him: but <u>the just shall live by his faith</u>."

Mark 4:35-41;

> "³⁵And the same day, when the even was come, he saith unto them, Let us pass over unto the other side. ³⁶And when they had sent away the multitude, they took him even as he was in the ship. And there were also with him other little ships. ³⁷And there arose a great storm of wind, and the waves beat into the ship, so that it was now full. ³⁸And he was in the hinder part of the ship, asleep on a pillow: and they awake him, and say unto him, Master, carest thou not that we perish? ³⁹And he arose, and rebuked the wind, and said unto the sea, Peace, be still. And the wind ceased, and there was a great calm. ⁴⁰And he said unto them, why are ye so fearful? How is it that ye have no faith? ⁴¹And they feared exceedingly, and said one to another, what manner of man is this, that even the wind and the sea obey him?"

Understanding the Working of Faith

1Timothy 6:12;

> "¹²Fight the good fight of faith, lay hold on eternal life, whereunto thou art also called, and hast professed a good profession before ᵐany witnesses."

The number one strategy (tactic) of the devil is to separate you from your faith, to keep us from making it to the other side, or to enjoy the blessing that is on the other side. We are to become masters of faith (subject of faith) so that our faith can work for us.

1 John 5:4;

> "⁴For whatsoever is born overcometh the world: and this is the victory that overcometh the world, even our faith."

In order to overcome the things that come against us, and the systems of the world it is imperative that we Understand the Workings of Faith.

Let us examine some examples that speak specifically about our faith:

1) The example of <u>two blind men</u> receiving their sight is in Matthew 9:29: "Then He touched their eyes, saying, "According to <u>your faith</u> let it be to you."
2) The example of the <u>Canaanite woman</u> receiving her daughter's deliverance is in Matthew 15:28: "Then Jesus answered and said to her, "O woman, great is <u>your faith!</u> Let it be to you as you desire." And her daughter was healed from that very hour."
3) The example the <u>woman with the issue of blood</u> receives her healing according to Mark 5:34, "And He said to her, "Daughter, <u>your faith</u> has made you well. Go in peace, and be healed of you affliction."

4) The example of a <u>blind man, Bartimeus,</u> receiving his sight can be found in Mark 10:52; "Then Jesus said to him, Go your way; <u>your faith</u> has made you well." And immediately he received his sight and followed Jesus on the road."

The following are examples of people who were rebuked because of unbelief or lack of faith:

Jesus rebuked his disciples because of their lack of faith is found in Matthew 17:20;

> "So Jesus said to them, "Because of your unbelief; for assuredly, I say to you, if you have faith as a mustard seed, you will say to this mountain, 'Move from here to there,' and it will move; and nothing will be impossible for you."

Jesus asking his disciples about their faith can be found in Luke 8:25:

> "He said to them, "Where is <u>your faith</u>?" And they were afraid, and marveled, saying to one another, "Who can this be? For He commands even the winds and water, and they obey Him!"

Peter being encouraged to be strong in faith:

Jesus encouraging Peter to be strong in faith is given in Luke 22:32;

> "But I have prayed for you, that <u>your faith</u> should not fail; and when you have returned to Me, strengthen your brethren."

Faith is your Servant – Again, a servant is a person who serves others, an individual who performs duties for his master whether they be personal or public matters.

Remember, it is imperative that we stay focused on the things of God and more importantly on the Word of God. What is happening in today's society, is the result of a demon-driven world system.

Paul is teaching us how operate in Faith. As a person of faith, it is important that we stay focused.

We find the following in According to 2 Corinthians 4:16-18;

> "¹⁶For which cause we faint not; but though our outward men perish, yet the inward man is renewed day by day. ¹⁷For our light affliction, which is but for a moment, worketh for us a far more exceeding and eternal weight of glory; ¹⁸While we look not at the things which are seen, but at the things which are not seen: for the things which are seen are temporal; but the things which are not seen are eternal."

Because it is talking about two men, the outward man (the flesh) and the inward man (the spirit).

In *2 Corinthians 4:16-18* tells us that the most important thing that we can do to develop or learn in life is to learn how to master our faith or how to use our faith, because everything in the kingdom of God is either accessed or activated by faith.

In *2 Corinthians 4:18*, we are not looking at the things which are seen, but rather look at the things that are of the Word of God.

Paul knows that these things are there: problems, sickness, financial issues, etc., are present, but we are not to focus on them, neither should we deny their existence. We don't deny that sickness exist, but God is telling us don't focus on it. Don't give it first place. Look at the things that are not seen, which are the promises of God; the things He has for your life.

Let's say that you are having a financial problem or something else that is taking your focus from God. What you have is something that is tangible (physical) and the five senses can pick it up. What Paul is asking is to not look at the physical. What we are to look at is something that is not seen with the senses, but that which is the Word of God; that which deals with your predicament a promise;

According to Philippians 4:19;

> "¹⁹But my God shall supply all your need according to his riches in glory by Christ Jesus"

The word, temporal, has to do with matter, things that are within this physical world, and things in this world that are subject to change. So things which are seen are subject to change. So everything that I can see, taste, touch, and smell are subject to change. But the things which are not seen, are eternal (The Word of God is ETERNAL).

So, what we are to do is replace what is seen with what is not seen, which is the Word of God or the Promise of God. Now the way to do this is to make sure that we are not looking at that which is seen. We should not give this first place. We should keep the Word of God in our <u>heart</u>, <u>mind</u>, <u>eyes,</u> and <u>ears</u>. The Word of God must constantly go into our spirit.

This is the part that a lot of Christians don't understand, because it takes discipline to put the flesh under, because the flesh wants to talk about how bad things are. What we need to learn is to put the Word of God in first place, and believe that the Word of God will change our circumstance, that is faith.

See Jesus is Lord, which means the Supreme Ruler, Jesus, and the Word of God, are one. So no matter what problem you have in your life, the Word of God is sufficient enough to change your situations.

Once again, remember Mark 4:35-41;

> "[35]And the same day, when the even was come, he saith they had sent away the multitude, they took him even as he was in the ship. And there were also with him other little ships. [37]And there arose a great storm of wind, and the waves beat into the ship, so that it was now full. [38]And he was in the hinder part of the ship, asleep on a pillow: and they awake him, and say unto him, Master, carest thou not that we perish? [39]And he arose, and rebuked the wind, and said unto the sea, Peace, be still. And the wind ceased, and there was a great calm. [40]And he said unto them, why are ye so fearful? How is it that ye have no faith? [41]And they feared exceedingly, and said one to another, what manner of man is this, that even the wind and the sea obey him?"

The storm was not sent by God to strength their faith, but was sent by the devil to separate them from their faith. You see what happened when they didn't keep their focus on the Word. They let the Word slip, fear came in, and fear replaced faith. Now, Satan had them where he wanted them, because he was out to destroy them. They woke Jesus up and He first spoke to the wind, and the sea, because the sea was raging. What we, as members of the church, need to understand is that we have the ability to deal with circumstances, situations and problems in the same way as Jesus. The root cause of the problem was the devil.

Remember that the number one strategy (premeditated plan) of the devil is to separate us from our faith because he knows we need faith in order to win our battles.

If we keep and holdfast to our faith satan knows that his defeat is imminent, because faith is designed to bring us the to victory in all situations, not just in one situation. So we are to hold on to our faith. This is where the challenge is because the flesh sometimes wants you to give in, but we have to stand firm and not waiver. The scripture says, "after all you have done stand!"

In Ephesians 6:13 tells us,

> "Wherefore take unto you the whole armor of God, that ye may be able to withstand in the evil day, and having done all, to stand."

Understanding the Working of Faith

Here is a situation according to *Mark 11:12-24;*

> "¹²And on the morrow, when they were come from Bethany, he was hungry: ¹³And seeing a fig tree afar off having leaves, he came, if haply he might find anything thereon: and when he came to it, he found nothing but leaves; for the time of figs was not yet. ¹⁴And Jesus answered and said unto it, No man eat fruit of thee hereafter forever. And his disciples heard it. ¹⁵And they come to Jerusalem: and Jesus went into the temple, and began to cast out them that sold and bought in the temple, and overthrew the tables of the oneychangers, and the seats of them that sold doves; ¹⁶And would not suffer that any man should carry any vessel through the temple. ¹⁷And he taught, saying unto them, Is it not written, My house shall be called of all nations the house of prayer? but ye have made it a den of thieves. ¹⁸And the scribes and chief priests heard it, and sought how they might destroy him: for they feared him, because all the people were astonished at his doctrine. ¹⁹And when even was come, he went out of the city. ²⁰And in the morning, as they passed by, they saw the fig tree dried up from the roots. ²¹And Peter calling to remembrance saith unto him, Master, behold, the fig tree which thou cursedst is withered away. ²²And Jesus answering saith unto them, Have faith in God. ²³For verily I say unto you, That whosoever shall say unto this mountain, Be thou removed, and be thou cast into the sea; and shall not doubt in his heart, but shall believe that those things which he saith shall come to pass; he shall have whatsoever he saith. ²⁴Therefore I say unto you, what things soever ye desire, when ye pray, believe that ye receive them, and ye shall have them.

Again, believing means an unqualified committal; it has to do with absolute trust in; it has to do with confidence that does not waiver; it has to do with selling out. We have said that many people have not seen faith work because they weren't sold out; believing means to sell out to God.

Many people think they can hang on to both sides of the fence and see faith work. They believe they can do a little of this and a little of that and faith will still work, but faith will not work without absolute trust. What we need to do is understand these things so our faith can work.

Let us continue with the gospel according to Mark 11, verses 19-22, **_Please note this is talking about having the God kind of FAITH!_** The God kind of faith is I believe it, I speak it, I expect something to happen. In the natural you see it first, then you believe it, but in the Kingdom of God I believe it first and then I see it.

The gospel, according to Mark 11 gives us some insight in verses 23-24. Now one thing that I want to talk about is the root. There was this tree that was dried up from the root. Most roots of a tree are under ground, but sometimes we may see some of the roots above the ground. We look at the roots as being the invisible realm, so the roots to the problem are in the invisible realm (spirit realm). Disease manifests itself in the physical, but its roots, its substance, in reality, is in the invisible realm (spirit realm).

What we are saying? We are saying that if we can curse the tree root, then it's going to dry up and die. If a person has cancer, then he should speak to that cancer.

When he releases his faith, his servant goes to the root of cancer, which is in the spirit realm and deal with the spirit of cancer. Once his servant has dealt with the spirit of cancer, it will no longer be a part of that his life.

Where does a tree get its sustenance? The tree gets it from the roots. The roots get it from the soil and feed it back up to the tree. So, if we cut the root, the tree can't be feed because it has to live on something. Therefore, when we believe with the God kind of faith and act on what we believe, we are releasing our Faith, our servant.

This needs to be said, because there are many believers who just believe, but believing alone won't get the job done. We can believe that if we eat food we won't die. But if we don't eat the food, we will die which is acting on what we believe.

So believing is not enough, we must act on what we believe, and when we act on what we believe that when we release our faith. So we can speak things and those things go to the root, because faith is designed and it is so forceful until it gets the job done.

Let's examine another key, because this is a very important. People say things and they are just speaking words, sounds. Words are not just sounds, they are Spirit, and the spirit of Faith is designed to get the job done.

Understanding the Working of Faith

Faith is a Servant of the believer. When Jesus spoke to the tree, you saw no physical evidence of change at that point. We look not at the things which are seen, but at the things which are not seen.

The next day when they can by the tree, Peter said master behold the tree that you cursed, has withered away, and Jesus said have faith in God or have the God kind of Faith.

According to *Genesis 1:1-26*, when God spoke *"let there be light"*, God released His faith in what He said. He believed that what He said was going to come to pass.

When He released those words, the Holy Spirit was hovering over the earth waiting to move, and when the word came, the Holy Spirit just manifested it. This is the same way in which we are designed. We were never designed to speak something that we don't want to come to pass. We have been talking and saying a lot of stuff and don't expect anything to happen, so we have no faith in our words.

Coming back to faith, we are people who are supposed to live by faith. This means that we are going to have to start watching our speech. We mention this, because this is a very important principle.

Paul said, *"Thou shall not doubt in your heart."* Remember that you can believe things in your heart that you can't believe with your head. *Romans 10:9-10* tells us that men believe with their hearts.

Summary

To believe with the heart means to believe with an independent of sense knowledge or evidence. It means to believe the Word of God, in spite of what might be going on around you. You must believe first, and then you act. You can't just act. Remember that you must have a two sided coin that was addressed in chapter 5. Now the Faith that has been released, has removed the tree.

Again, we must understand that faith is our servant that has been given unto us by our loving Heavenly Father. As we have been blessed with this wonderful servant, let us learn to use Him, we are co-laborer with God to get His will done in expanding His Kingdom.

Confession

PLEASE READ THIS CONFESSION ALOUD SO THAT THE OUTER EAR CAN HEAR, SO WE CAN BELIEVE SO THAT OUR FAITH WILL INCREASE. AS HUMAN BEINGS, WE PROCESS THINGS AS FOLLOWS: WE THINK IT, WE SAY IT, AND WE DO IT. BUT WITH GOD, WE KNOW THAT FAITH COMETH BY HEARING AND HEARING BY THE WORD OF GOD. WHEN WE FOLLOW THIS PRINCIPLE, WE WILL BE ABLE TO WALK IT OUT.

Jesus is the High Priest of my confession, I hold fast to my confession of faith. I decide to walk by faith and practice faith. My faith comes by hearing and hearing by the Word of God. Jesus is the author and the developer of my faith. I take my shield of faith and quench every fiery dart that the wicked one brings against me. I am a believer and not a doubter. I am the just, I live by faith, and I please my Heavenly Father. I am born of God; I have the victory over the world systems because I am a person of faith.

9. Faith is Your Servant
Part 2

There are two categories of faith within the God kind of faith. Number one is creative faith and number two is dominating faith.

Let's look at both of these:

According to *Hebrews 11:1-4;*

> "¹Now faith is the substance of things hoped for, the evidence of things not seen."

Notice what it calls faith, *"a substance"*, and notice in verses 3-4, the writer is not just saying that we exercise our faith to believe that God spoke the world into existence. That's not what he means, that is not the main focus here. In verse 3, he is saying unto us this is the way that God did it. God did it by faith. He didn't use any bricks, mortar, wood, or no such thing; it was faith. It was faith, faith is the substance that He used to speak the world it into existence.

When God spoke the earth into existence, according to *Genesis 1:1-26*, notice that God had to say something, because He believed in His heart, and then he had to speak it with His mouth; He had to act on what He believed. Now when you believe something independent of sense knowledge or evidence, it may not be like you want it to be, but in your heart we know how we want it, and so we release how we want it, and believe how we want it to come to pass.

When God spoke the world into existence, it was a new creation. It was something fresh; it was not something worn out or revamped. It was something new. Here, we are talking about creative faith. This is the same type of faith (God Kind of Faith) that is in the Word of God.

According to Romans 12:3;

> "³For I say, through the grace given unto me, to every man that is among you, not to think of himself more highly than he ought to think; but to think soberly, according as God hath dealt to every man the measure of faith (**The God Kind of Faith**)." Emphases add.

Faith is deposited into our heart when we are born-again. As a citizen of the Kingdom of God, a child of God that has been transferred into the Kingdom of God, that know the time and place when we received the Lord Jesus Christ as their own personal Lord and Savior, we are not talking about when you got water baptized.

We have two categories of faith within the God kind of faith. Number one is creative faith and number two is dominating faith.

Let's look at both of them. Jesus operated in both of these categories. But before we go to the New Testament, let us look at another example in the Old Testament.

Understanding the Working of Faith

According to 2 Kings 5:1–15,

"¹Now Naaman, captain of the host of the king of Syria, was a great man with his master, and honourable, because by him the LORD had given deliverance unto Syria: he was also a mighty man in valour, but he was a leper. ²And the Syrians had gone out by companies, and had brought away captive out of the land of Israel a little maid; and she waited on Naaman's wife. ³And she said unto her mistress, Would God my lord were with the prophet that is in Samaria! for he would recover him of his leprosy. ⁴And one went in, and told his lord, saying, Thus and thus said the maid that is of the land of Israel. ⁵And the king of Syria said, Go to, go, and I will send a letter unto the king of Israel. And he departed, and took with him ten talents of silver, and six thousand pieces of gold, and ten changes of raiment. ⁶And he brought the letter to the king of Israel, saying, Now when this letter is come unto thee, behold, I have therewith sent Naaman my servant to thee, that thou mayest recover him of his leprosy. ⁷And it came to pass, when the king of Israel had read the letter, that he rent his clothes, and said, Am I God, to kill and to make alive, that this man doth send unto me to recover a man of his leprosy? Wherefore consider, I pray you, and see how he seeketh a quarrel against me. ⁸And it was so, when Elisha the man of God had heard that the king of Israel had rent his clothes, that he sent to the king, saying, Wherefore hast thou rent thy clothes? let him come now to me, and he shall know that there is a prophet in Israel. ⁹So Naaman came with his horses and with his chariot, and stood at the door of the house of Elisha. ¹⁰And Elisha sent a messenger unto him, saying, Go and wash in Jordan seven times, and thy flesh shall come again to thee, and thou shalt be clean.

> ¹¹But Naaman was worth, and went away, and said, Behold, I thought, He will surely come out to me, and stand, and call on the name of the LORD his God, and strike his hand over the place, and recover the leper. ¹²Are not Abana and Pharpar, rivers of Damascus, better than all the waters of Israel? May I not wash in them, and be clean? So he turned and went away in a rage. ¹³And his servants came near, and spake unto him, and said, My father, if the prophet had bid thee do some great thing, wouldest thou not have done it? how much rather then, when he saith to thee, Wash, and be clean? ¹⁴Then went he down, and dipped himself seven times in Jordan, according to the saying of the man of God: and his flesh came again like unto the flesh of a little child, and he was clean. ¹⁵And he returned to the man of God, he and all his company, and came, and stood before him: and he said, Behold, now I know that there is no God in all the earth, but in Israel: now therefore, I pray thee, take a blessing of thy servant."

In this example, when Naaman was cured of leprosy, starting at verse 8-15, notice what God did, He created new flesh on him, and the flesh that He created was the best (flesh like a young child).

This is just one example, let's see another one.

According to John 2:1-11;

> "And the third day there was a marriage in Cana of Galilee; and the mother of Jesus was there: ²And both Jesus was called, and his disciples, to the marriage. ³And when they wanted wine, the mother of Jesus saith unto him, They have no wine. ⁴Jesus saith unto her, Woman, what have I to do with thee? mine hour is not yet come. ⁵His mother saith unto the servants, Whatsoever he saith unto you, do it.

> ⁶And there were set there six waterpots of stone, after the manner of the purifying of the Jews, containing two or three firkins apiece. ⁷Jesus saith unto them, Fill the waterpots with water. And they filled them up to the brim. ⁸And he saith unto them, Draw out now, and bear unto the governor of the feast. And they bare it. ⁹When the ruler of the feast had tasted the water that was made wine, and knew not whence it was: (but the servants which drew the water knew;) the governor of the feast called the bridegroom, ¹⁰And saith unto him, Every man at the beginning doth set forth good wine; and when men have well drunk, then that which is worse: but thou hast kept the good wine until now. ¹¹This beginning of miracles did Jesus in Cana of Galilee, and manifested forth his glory; and his disciples believed on him."

In this example, we see Jesus creating new wine. This wine that Jesus created was not moonshine, but was the best. This was a creative miracle. This same creative power, we have throughout the word of God. This kind of faith is a servant we have from our Heavenly Father; see Faith is a servant to the believers.

Dominating Faith

The second category of faith is Dominating Faith; this type of faith enables us to dominate situations, circumstances, and problems. We can dominate what has been created, with Dominating Faith, if something gets out of line, we can put it back in line. We have domain over demonic forces and anything that the Satan tries to do or bring against us.

Remember that we are still talking about believing and acting on the Word of God. In both of these examples, they had to act on the Word of God.

In order for the Word of God to work, we shouldn't say, *"I just couldn't believe it."* This is the problem with many Christians today. They are trying to get God to move when they have never acted on the Word of God. You see, we've got to do it God's way, because no other way is going to work.

Most Christians don't understand the working of Faith. They try to play it safe just in case God's way doesn't work. God is not going to let you play it safe. The Word of God works and we are going to work it.

Remember my list back in Chapter 5? Faith and Belief are not the same. One reason I believe that the $2,500.00 dollars was manifested, was because I didn't have a backup plan. If the Word of God didn't work, we probably wouldn't be around to write this book. I stepped out on God's WORD, but what if He hadn't come through, who knows what might have happened?

I truly believe this is where God wants all His children to be, out there where they are totally trusting in Him.

Faith requires us put our soul and body under the control of our spirit.

An example of dominating Faith:

According to Matthew 14:24-31;

> "24But the ship was now in the midst of the sea, tossed with waves: for the wind was contrary 25And in the fourth watch of the night Jesus went unto them, walking on the sea. 26And when the disciples saw him walking on the sea, they were troubled, saying, It is a spirit; and they cried out for fear. 27But straightway Jesus spake unto them, saying, Be of good cheer; it is I; be not afraid. 28And Peter answered him and said, Lord, if it be thou, bid me come unto thee on the water. 29And he said, Come. And when Peter was come down out of the ship, he walked on the water, to go to Jesus. 30But when he saw the wind boisterous, he was afraid; and beginning to sink, he cried, saying, Lord, save me. 31And immediately Jesus stretched forth his hand, and caught him, and said unto him, O thou of little faith, wherefore didst thou doubt?"

Peter believed and demonstrated it by getting out of the boat and walking on the water. It says, "But when he saw the wind boisterous, he was afraid; and beginning to sink, he cried, saying, "Lord save me."

Now what did Peter do? In going from the boat to Jesus, he took his eyes off Jesus (The Word of God), and put his eyes on his circumstances.

Now the Bible says something that is very subtle, *"and beginning to sink."* Let me ask a question? How do you begin to sink? If you are in the water, how do you begin to sink?

Remember *Hebrews 11:1;*

> "1Now faith is the substance of things hoped for, the evidence of things not seen"

I am going to step out there with this statement, "I believe faith becomes whatever it needs to be in order to get the job done the right way in line with the Word of God. Faith was the substance that was holding Peter up while he was walking on the water, as long as he kept his eyes on Jesus (The Word of God).

Peter obviously didn't just drop out of sight under the water, but it was a slow process because the scripture says Peter was beginning to sink. The reason that he was beginning to sink, was the devil created circumstances (the wind being boisterous) causing Peter to be distracted while trying to reach his destination. The devil will cause circumstances in your life to distract (sidetrack\divert) you and separate you from your faith, in order to keep you from reaching your destiny.

Have you been around people who talk against the plan of God for your life, or talk against a project that you are working on?

I remember when I started my ministries, there were some people, I thought, were working with me as I was striving to do the things that God had called me to do.

Then I noticed that they were saying that did not support what support the plan that God had for me. I made a mental note, and when I heard them say the same thing for a third time, I knew they were not in agreement in helping to accomplish what God had given me to do. You see, sometimes the devil will send people to separate you from your faith, so that you can't fulfill the vision that God has given you.

I remember when I was having a book signing and promoting my book *What God's Love Got To Do With It?* Someone made the statement, "you and your little book." I noticed it right away that this person was not supportive of what I was doing. I concluded that they were being used by the devil to plant a seed to hinder, or separate me from my faith, so that I wouldn't be able accomplish what God desired me to accomplish.

Again, the longer you look at your circumstances, the more they can drain you of your faith; just like a car's battery that can be drained. This is what was happening to Peter. The longer he looked at the storm, the more he was sinking; being drained of his faith. That is why the scripture says, "and he began to sink".

Peter had faith, but doubt creped in. Therefore Peter had a hole in His faith, and it was draining out, so He couldn't make to Jesus.

The supernatural, that believers are meant to walk in, cannot be done, if you can't do the things that you are supposed to do as a believer. This means that you are sinking because you are looking at your circumstances.

Remember, according to 2 Corinthians 4:18;

> "18While we look not at the things which are seen, but at The things which are not seen: for the things which are seen are temporal; but the things which are not seen are eternal."

Peter was walking on the Word of God. The Word of God dominates natural laws, and if you have the Word of God in you, you can walk on the Word of God. You can do things that natural people cannot do. We are designed to do works.

According to John 14:12;

> "Verily, verily, I say unto you, He that believeth on me, the works that I do shall he do also; and greater works than these shall he do; because I go unto my Father."

According to 2 Corinthians 4:13;

> "We having the same spirit of faith, according as it is written, I believed, and therefore have I spoken; we also believe, and therefore speak."

God has things that He wants us to do, and He wants us to standout, not so much that people can see how great we are, but so that people can see how great He is.

He is going to give you something that is beyond the normal; you already have something in you called potential. Peter was a man of faith, and that's why Jesus liked Peter. He may not have been the coolest disciple, but he was a person of faith.

God delights in His children when they step out with nothing but His Word under their feet. God delights in us when we "get out of that boat", out of that comfort zone, out of that place that we are familiar with and step into a zone that we've got nothing to hold us up except the Word of God. If we don't step out on our faith, we are apt to fail.

God delights when believers do this, because this is when faith works its best. Jesus knew when He spoke to the tree it was going to obey Him, because He had no doubt in His heart. Jesus saw Himself as a ruler and not as the one being ruled. When He told the tree to do something, it was going to do it.

Something is very interesting about the tree we find in Mark 11 verse 19. This tree could very well represent the circumstances that Satan brings in our life when we step out on the Word of God.

Why? Because he comes to get our faith and if we look at our circumstances too long, they will slowly drain our faith. Now what we need to do is feed our faith daily.

We can start by reading something that will feed our faith. Our faith need to be fed, just like our body needs to be fed every day. Faith comes by hearing and hearing the Word of God. This should be a constant each day of our lives.

We, as believers, have not been applying the supernatural as we should, because we don't "*Understand The Workings of Faith*". First, you must be a believer. Once you are born-again you, have the measure of faith.

What we need to do is get specific promises and feed our faith. As our faith grows, we can began to speak the things of God and they will come to pass. As we continue to do this we will began to rise above the things that has hinder or hold us back. We will move from being overcome by the problems and circumstances of life to being an over comer by faith.

According to: 1 John 5:4;

> "⁴For whatsoever is born overcometh the world: and this is the victory that overcometh the world, even our faith."

We have access to and the power to activate the promise by faith.

According to Romans 5:1-3;

> "Therefore being justified by faith, we have peace with God through our Lord Jesus Christ: ²By whom also we have access by faith into this grace wherein we stand, and rejoice in hope of the glory of God. ³And not only so, but we glory in tribulations also: knowing that tribulation worketh patience."

According to *Matthew 9:27-31;*

> "²⁷And when Jesus departed thence, two blind men followed him, crying, and saying, Thou son of David, have mercy on us. ²⁸And when he was come into the house, the blind men came to him: and Jesus saith unto them, Believe ye that I am able to do this? They said unto him, Yea, Lord. ²⁹Then touched he their eyes, saying, According to your faith be it unto you. ³⁰And their eyes were opened; and Jesus strictly charged them, saying, See that no man know it. ³¹But they, when they were departed, spread abroad his fame in all that country."

Notice in this potion of scripture we have two things that are together, one, belief and second, faith. In verse 28 Jesus said unto them, "Believe ye that I am able to do this?" And in *verse 29, Jesus said unto them, according to your faith, be it unto you."*

Faith is an action!

Please understand that believing is depending on God's ability and not our own. When we believe with our head and depend on something that we can do based on our experiences, we are limited in what we can do. But believing with our heart is much bigger than that. It takes us into a realm that is beyond our natural ability.

Faith is the currency of the kingdom, and we need faith to transfer that which we need or desire. It works just like money. In the natural, the only thing that stands between us and what we need or desire, and everything else is money. Money seems to be the main ingredient that separates us from those things in the natural.

Faith works in the same way, except on a totally different dimension. We use faith like currency and just like currency, if you don't have enough faith, there are some things that you cannot get. It is imperative that we first understand that we have been given the measure of faith, and the second thing we must understand is that faith can grow.

We must exercise our faith so that it can grow. The more we use (exercise) our faith the stronger it becomes. The third thing we must know is that there is no limit to how strong our faith can become. Not only that, but our faith can be so develop that it becomes or operates with precision.

According to Mark 11:23;

> "²³For verily I say unto you, that whosoever shall say unto this mountain, Be thou removed, and be thou cast into the sea; and shall not doubt in his heart, but shall believe that those things which he saith shall come to pass; he shall have whatsoever he saith."

Jesus said you can say unto this mountain be thou removed. There may be other mountains, but your faith can be so developed that it brings in exactly what you want it to bring in, and when you want it to be manifested. We should be able to believe God, so that Faith causes what we want to come in when we want it to come.

There is one last illustration I need to share, to help us clearly understand that Faith is our Servant.

According to Luke 17: 5-10, (NLT)

> "⁵The apostles said to the Lord, "Show us how to increase our faith." ⁶The Lord answered, "If you had faith even as small as a mustard seed, you could say to this mulberry tree, May you be uprooted and thrown into the sea,' and it would obey you! ⁷When a servant comes in from plowing or taking care of sheep, does his master say, 'Come in and eat with me'? ⁸No, he says, 'Prepare my meal, put on your apron, and serve me while I eat. Then you can eat later.' ⁹And does the master thank the servant for doing what he was told to do? of course not. ¹⁰ n the same way, when you obey me you should say, 'we are unworthy servants who have simply done our duty.'"

Here, within the Holy Scriptures we read that when the disciples asked for more faith, Jesus replied that faith is like a servant.

Summary

We have shared that faith is a servant. Please don't shift you attention to looking at what a person's faith has done, by saying by my faith I have gotten me this or that. Remember that faith is a gift from our loving Heavenly Father, and no gift is greater than the one who gives it.

Remember we must understand that faith is our servant that it has been given unto us by our loving heavenly Father. As we have been blessed with a wonderful servant, let us learn to use Him as we co-laborer with God to get His will done in expanding the Kingdom of God.

Confession

PLEASE READ THIS CONFESSION ALOUD SO THAT THE OUTER EAR CAN HEAR, SO WE CAN BELIEVE SO THAT OUR FAITH WILL INCREASE. AS HUMAN BEINGS, WE PROCESS THINGS AS FOLLOWS: WE THINK IT, WE SAY IT, AND WE DO IT. BUT WITH GOD, WE KNOW THAT FAITH COMETH BY HEARING AND HEARING BY THE WORD OF GOD. WHEN WE FOLLOW THIS PRINCIPLE, WE WILL BE ABLE TO WALK IT OUT.

Jesus is the High Priest of my confession, I hold fast to my confession of faith. I decide to walk by faith and practice faith. My faith comes by hearing and hearing by the Word of God. Jesus is the author and the developer of my faith. I take my shield of faith and quench every fiery dart that the wicked one brings against me. I am a believer and not a doubter. I am the just, I live by faith, and I please my Heavenly Father. I am born of God; I have the victory over the world systems because I am a person of faith.

10. Examples of Individuals Possessing STRONG Faith

In this chapter, I wish to share examples of individual that were strong in faith.

The Faith of Noah

An overview of Noah's Faith can be found in Genesis chapters 5 through 10 and Hebrews 11:7, (NKJV) "by faith Abraham, when he was tested, offered up Isaac and he who had received the promises offered up his only begotten son"

Let's break down this verse and look at the individual parts:

Applying faith, Noah listened to and believed the divine warning from God of things not yet seen.

In verse 1, we read that faith deals with the unseen. This is the case with Noah. He is warned of things not yet seen. There is some debate as to exactly what is meant *"by the things which Noah had not yet seen."* Some believe he had never seen rain, and there is some scriptural evidence to support this possibility. One thing we are absolutely certain about is "he had never seen."

Genesis 6:11-12;

> "all the fountains of the great deep were broken up, and the windows of heaven were opened. 12 And the rain was on the earth forty days and forty nights. 13 The end of all flesh has come before Me, for the earth is filled with violence through them; and behold I will destroy them with the earth."

Noah had never seen global destruction. God's warning to him was that He would destroy the world.

God is telling Noah something that stretches the imagination to the breaking point. Millions of people are going to die. ALL people are going to die. All animal life will be extinguished. The waters will cover the highest hills. Nothing will be left.

This is the judgment of God upon unceasing, rampant, pervasive, global wickedness. A line has been crossed, and God is going to fix the problem because "the wickedness of man was great in the earth, and every intent of the thoughts of his heart was only evil continually" (Genesis 6:6).

By Faith, Noah feared God.

How do we know Noah feared God? First, the Greek word for "fear" is only used twice in the New Testament. A closely related word used twice is translated "devout." Which means sincere, genuine, not hypocritical.

Genesis 6:9;

> describes Noah by saying he ". . . was a just man, perfect in his generations. Noah walked with God."

That is the same phrase used to describe Enoch. He was an observably righteous man. One translation says he was blameless. The following are evidences of the fear of God:

By Faith, Noah prepared an Ark.

Temptation tests our fear of God. Sin proves our lack of fear. But the unmistakable proof of Noah's fear of God was his faithful obedience in performing a gargantuan task in the face of a thoroughly evil generation. Noah believed God's unbelievable warning. "One of the greatest practical acts of faith in all history was Noah's cutting down the first gopher tree for wood to make the ark." He built a boat with three decks that was 450' by 75' by 45' over a period of 100 years, with hand tools. That is perseverance.

It required patient, long-term faith to persevere like that. Not only was Noah initially convinced that God had spoken, but he was convinced of it for 100 years! That takes faith.

> Genesis 6:22; *"According to all that God commanded him, so he did"*

By Faith, Noah saved eight souls from destruction.

The faith of the one had a sanctifying effect on all the others. God warned Noah to save himself and his household by preparing the ark.

Suppose he had not been a man of faith? Not only would he have lost his own life, but the lives of his family members. We wouldn't be here to talk about it, nor would we have a Savior in the Lord Jesus. Is it not astounding that the fate of the entire world depended, in a sense, upon the Faith of this one man?

By Faith, Noah condemned the world.

Because of his unshakable Faith in God's word, Noah's devout and upright life was a continued testimony against the complete godlessness of the culture around him. Notice that when we are discouraged at the state of things surrounding us, we still have a church family with which to fellowship.

We have others with whom we can talk about the greatness of God. We can gather together for corporate worship, and we rejoice in the blessing of being with like minded believers.

The Genesis account says nothing about the spiritual condition of Noah's wife or their sons or daughters-in-law.

We do not know how much of an encouragement or discouragement they were to Noah in this weird, seemingly never ending project. The Bible does not speak to it either way. But it does consistently present Noah as the righteous one, the man of faith. It seems as though he may have been completely alone in his belief that God would soon destroy the world.

Let me share from Charles Spurgeon's words about this: "Noah believed through a hundred and twenty solitary years! It was a long martyrdom. Our life is quite long enough for the trial of faith. Even if a man lives to be eighty, and has sixty years of that life spent in the exercise of faith, it is only by almighty grace that he holds out. Noah lived two of our lives in this way.

If a little flood had happened and moved his ark a little, he would have had some evidence for his faith; but there was no flood at all; and his ark lay high and dry for a century and a quarter! How few could endure this! Yonder dear friend has been praying for the last six months, and the Lord has not heard him, and he begins to doubt whether the Lord does hear prayer at all. You are not much like Noah.

By Faith, Noah inherited the righteousness of Christ.

You can hardly believe for one hundred and twenty days. "Alas!" says one, "I have prayed for my husband these twenty years!" It is a long time to wait; but what would you do with a hundred added on to it?

Years made Noah's faith more mature, and less feeble. This grey father of the age went on with his preaching, went on with his intercession, and, without a doubt, waited for God in his own time to justify his servant before the eyes of men." 4

Finally, the writer of Hebrews reinforces what the New Testament teaches elsewhere; salvation is a gift. Because Noah believed God's warning, God credited it to him as righteousness, in the same fashion as He did for Abraham.

Listen again to Hebrews 11:7; "By faith Noah, being warned of God of things not seen as yet, moved with fear, prepared an ark to the saving of his house; by the which he condemned the world, and became heir of the righteousness which is by faith."

Noah received "the righteousness which is according to faith." Righteousness is a gift, not an accomplishment. Heirs are granted an inheritance, not because they deserve it, but because the owner of the inheritance desires to grant it to another, usually a child.

The writer is saying that there is a righteousness that the children of God inherit because they have faith in God. They believe what He says, they do what He commands, and they are granted an inheritance: perfect righteousness.

In other words, like Noah, when we believe God's word, we inherit salvation. God grants us total forgiveness of all our sins, and He grants us total righteousness, as though we had never sinned. This may be even more amazing than being told God is going to destroy the entire world because of sin with a global flood!

That seems more believable than the promise that all who trust Jesus the Christ, have a Savior from the wrath of God.

In Genesis 7, verse 1, God said to Noah, *"Come into the ark."* He did not say, "Go into the ark." In a similar fashion, Jesus says to sinners, "Come to Me, all you who labor and are heavy laden, and I will give you rest."

If you are burdened by the guilt of sin, if you are tired of trying to save yourself by your own efforts, if you are ready to place the burden of your salvation upon Christ, then He says "COME." Take Him at His word. That is the faith that saves.

B. The Faith of Abraham

An overview Abraham the Father of Faith, according Genesis chapters 17 through 25;

According to Hebrews 11:17-18;

> "*17By faith Abraham, when he was tried, offered up Isaac: and he that had received the promises offered up his only begotten son, 18Of whom it was said, That in Isaac shall thy seed be called:*"

Abraham is without question one of the outstanding individuals of the Old Testament. God spoke to him personally, actually visited him in his home and even considered him a friend. And Abraham loved God.

He obeyed him, served him, and was even willing to sacrifice his son to prove his faith. Abraham is a biblical superhero, richly deserving a place in the Old Testament Hall of Faith. But are his experiences something you can personally relate to?

Abraham may seem superhuman, but if we look more closely at some of the incidents in his life, we see someone who is like the rest of us, with many frailties and weaknesses. He eventually became a man who believed.

> Genesis 15:6; "believed the Lord, and he credited it to him as righteousness."

Abraham wasn't born this way. He had to grow and learn by experience. In Genesis 12, God told Abraham to uproot himself and his family from their familiar surroundings and move to a new land.

It was a test of faith and obedience for a 75-year-old man; Abraham simply did as he was told. He went out, *"even though he did not know where he was going"* (*Hebrews 11:8*). On this occasion, Abraham trusted God. But Abraham wasn't perfect.

Read the rest of Genesis 12. Isn't this a rather strange thing for a man of faith to have done? Abraham's wife, Sarah, even at her age, was so attractive that other men were taken with her beauty.

Abraham was concerned that some might even consider killing him so that Sarah would be available to marry. Fearing for his life, Abraham deceived Pharaoh into believing his beautiful wife was his sister.

Earlier, Abraham had trusted God. But in this one chapter we see Abraham acting first in faith, and then in fear. Even though Abraham was a man of faith, he was an imperfect human.

Read the accounts of Abraham's relationship with his nephew, Lot. Note how Abraham preferred peace to strife in the incident recorded in *Genesis 13:5-12*. Lot took advantage of his uncle's desire for peace, and chose what he thought was the best territory. It was a decision that rebounded. Lot and his family settled in a disputed area and became caught up in local wars. In *Genesis 14:12-16*, Lot was taken prisoner, and we read how Abraham went to his rescue.

Abraham's love of peace, mixed with loyalty and courage, is an impressive quality. He was indeed a man learning to live up to God's standards. But he had not yet fully learned to trust in God.

God had made important promises to Abraham regarding his descendants. The problem was, Abraham didn't yet have any descendants. Sarah was barren, and she and Abraham were well past the age they could expect to have children.

In *Genesis 15:1-3*, Abraham explained this situation to God. But God patiently insisted that eventually they would have a son who would inherit the promises.

C. The Faith of Moses

An overview Moses, the Father of Faith, according Exodus chapter 2 through Deuteronomy 34;

The life of Moses illustrates clearly why Faith is of supreme worth. It leads to action. Knowledge, sentiment, God's call, God's instructions and even God's grace will not lead to action without faith. It does remove mountains.

Faith is the active, transforming and conquering quality behind effective Christian service. "Faith without works is indeed dead."

(1) Perception, backed up by Faith, results in resourcefulness.

Moses' parents were perceptive. They saw that he was no ordinary child.

In *Hebrews 11:23*,

> *"23By faith Moses, when he was born, was hid three months of his parents, because they saw he was a proper child; and they were not afraid of the king's commandment."*

According to *Hebrews 11:24*, Moses' parents ignored the edict of Pharaoh and hid the baby for three months. It also made them resourceful.

They devised a plan, a very cunning plan, whereby the baby would be adopted and enjoy the protection of Pharaoh's daughter and yet be nurtured by his own mother acting as his nurse.

In *Exodus 2:3-10* tells us, "Moses' parents were intelligent and their scheme was a good one. However, it entailed uncertainties, risks and dangers. There was no guarantee that it would succeed. Faith overcame their doubts and fears. Faith put the plan into operation. The child was saved by faith.

It is a good thing to be intelligent. We need to be perceptive and to have insight, to anticipate problems and have solutions. However that is not enough in itself. Faith is needed to put ideas into practice.

(2) Sympathy allied with Faith results in a professed allegiance:

Moses was nurtured by his mother and in those early years, he learned all the important stories about the patriarchs of his people. As he grew, his sympathies lay with the children of Israel. However, he could have been sympathetic to his people's plight but remained the adopted son of Pharaoh's daughter.

He could have shed tears in private over their oppression and lowly status but continued to enjoy the pleasures of Egypt.

In *Hebrews 11:24-26*, Faith transformed his sympathy into active allegiance. He refused to be known as the son of Pharaoh's daughter.

He chose to be ill-treated along with the people of God rather than to enjoy the pleasures of sin for a short time. He regarded disgrace for the sake of Christ as of greater value than the treasures of Egypt, because he was looking ahead to his reward.

These are stirring words. They convey, vividly, something about the sacrifice that Moses made. He did so deliberately by faith. He refused, he chose and he looked ahead. Moses lost status, abandoned pleasure and renounced material rewards. He did so because he hoped to deliver his people from slavery - he was looking ahead to his reward - to the Promised Land.

Moses eventually sets his people free because by faith, he regarded disgrace of greater value than the treasures of Egypt.

(3) Faith kept Moses in his calling till the work was done.

Moses could never question his calling. Yet in spite of God appearing in a burning bush and giving him clear instructions Moses was reluctant to get started. By faith, he finally started out for Egypt and by faith, he persevered in the task God had called him to.

It was not easy for Moses to persevere. His task was to secure the release of the Israelites and lead them out of Egypt to the Promised Land.

To achieve this, he and Aaron had to negotiate with Pharaoh. As plague followed plague, Pharaoh came to hate the sight of Moses. After the plague of darkness, according to *Exodus 10:28*, Pharaoh said to Moses, "*Get out of my sight*! Make sure you do not appear before me again! The day you see my face you will die."

It was not long before Moses was in Pharaoh's presence again. His life was relatively safe because Moses, himself, was highly regarded in Egypt by Pharaoh's officials and by the people.

According to *Exodus 10:27*, Moses had to announce the tenth plague; the death of the first born in the land. By this time he was heartily sick of the struggle and the terrible consequence of Pharaoh's intransigence. We read that Moses, hot with anger, left Pharaoh.

According to *Exodus 11:8*, no one likes to be the bearer of bad news. No one enjoys being hated. No one relishes prolonged confrontation. Moses persevered because he had faith in God's word. By faith he succeeded, by faith the people left Egypt and were delivered from slavery to freedom.

We need faith to overcome opposition. Today in the West too many Christians wilt in the face of opposition. Courage, steadfastness and militancy are not fashionable virtues. Perhaps the hardest thing that Moses had to bear was opposition from his own people.

The Israelites said to him before they crossed the Red Sea, according to Exodus, "Didn't we say to you in Egypt, 'Leave us alone; let us serve the Egyptians'?"

(4) Moses and the Israelites carefully followed the instructions they were given by Faith.

Moses and his people kept the Passover just as they were told to. No short cuts were taken; there were no omissions or modifications.

God's instructions were followed to the letter. We read, according *Exodus 12:28*, the Israelites did just what the LORD commanded Moses and Aaron.

All those who obeyed God were delivered from the angel of death. According to *Exodus 12:23* when the LORD goes through the land to strike down the Egyptian's, "he will see the blood on the top and sides of the door-frame and will pass over that doorway, and he will not permit the destroyer to enter your houses and strike you down"

By Faith Moses and the Israelites did the only thing they could in extremity - they went forward.

Pharaoh had second thoughts about losing his cheap labor force and sent out an army to round up the Israelites and bring them back to Egypt. When the enemy got near and danger threatened God provided a way of escape.

All the Israelites had to do was go forward to benefit from God's provision. It wasn't so easy. I expect some found it a scary experience to walk between those two, parallel, walls of water. On they went, on to the other side and safety.

As the writer to the *Hebrews 12:3* (NIV) stated

> *"Consider him who endured such opposition from sinful men, so that you will not grow weary and lose heart."*

This is the very best of advice. We see in the story of Moses and the Exodus many, many, manifestations of God's grace. God does not want his people ever to forget the grace that brought them out of Egypt.

We also see in that story the indispensable nature of faith. Without it, notwithstanding God's grace, there would have been no deliverance. It is the active principle in the deliverance of God's people. The Israelites were released from slavery and set free to journey to the Promised Land by grace and through faith.

Faith remains the active principle in the deliverance of God's people. It sets God's people free. It keeps God's people travelling upward to Zion, the beautiful city of God.

D. The Faith of David

An overview David life according to 1 Samuel through 2 Chronicles; God directed Samuel to go to the abode of Jesse, where he would anoint a king from among Jesse's sons. According to 1 Samuel 16:6, Samuel did as he was told, then began to take stock of each son. "So it was, when they came, that he looked at Eliab and said, 'Surely the LORD has anointed is before Him." Samuel reasoned the way so many of us do. He was certain that Jesse's oldest son, Eliab, with his confident bearing, height and impressive good looks, was the one God would choose.

According to *1 Samuel 16:7*,

> *"But the LORD said to Samuel; "Do not look at his appearance or at his physical stature, because I have refused him.*

> *For the LORD does not see as man sees; for man looks at the outward appearance, but the LORD looks at the heart."*

One by one Jesse's sons came before Samuel to determine who was to be king. It didn't occur to Jesse to send for young David. Samuel was puzzled as it became evident God had chosen none of the sons brought to him.

"Are all the young men here?" he asked (*1 Samuel 16:11 13*). Informed that the youngest was out tending sheep, Samuel requested: "Send and bring him. For we will not sit down till he comes here And the LORD said, 'Arise, anoint him; for this is the one!

Then Samuel took the horn of oil and anointed him in the midst of his brothers; and the Spirit of the LORD came upon David from that day forward."

As the youngest of eight sons of Jesse, David's job was to tend sheep. Sheepherding meant lonely vigils, as well as opportunities to get to know God in an intimate relationship. This intimate relationship with God developed throughout David's life.

From these humble beginnings came Israel's greatest king. David's early training had taught him to herd sheep; now God would teach him to lead a nation. After his anointing as king, David returned to his flocks. It was from here that he visited his brothers on the Philistine battlefield and witnessed Goliath's challenge.

When David asked what would happen to the man who slew this insufferable braggart, someone reported David's words to King Saul, and the king sent for him. David wasn't intimidated by Israel's king or the enemy giant.

He recounted how he had killed a lion and a bear that had threatened his family's sheep, "and this uncircumcised Philistine will be like one of them, seeing he has defied the armies of the living God ... The LORD, who delivered me from the paw of the lion and from the paw of the bear, He will deliver me from the hand of this Philistine." (*1 Samuel 17:36*).

Carrying only his staff, David marched forward to meet the giant, stopping only to select five smooth stones from a brook. When Goliath saw how small young David was, he mocked him:

> *"Am I a dog that you come to me with sticks? ... Come to me, and I will give your flesh to the birds of the air and the beasts of the field!" (Verses 43-44)*

David's response was fearless: "You come to me with a sword, with a spear, and with a javelin. But I come to you in the name of the LORD of hosts, the God of the armies of Israel, whom you have defied. This day the LORD will deliver you into my hand, and I will strike you and take your head from you.

This day I will give the carcasses of the camp of the Philistines to the birds of the air and the wild beasts of the earth, that all the earth may know that there is a God in Israel" (verses 45-46). The following events quickly found their way into legend.

David rushed toward the giant.

> "Then David put his hand in his bag and took out a stone; and he slung it and struck the Philistine in his forehead, so that the stone sank into his forehead, and he fell on his face to the earth. So David prevailed over the Philistine with a sling and a stone, and struck the Philistine and killed him." (Verses 49-50)

David's accomplishments were many. He captured Jerusalem, making it the national capital, and reunited the nation. In a 40-year span he controlled an empire that stretched from Egypt to Mesopotamia. A man of many talents, he was a shepherd, poet, musician, warrior and statesman, and an administrator who set a standard for the later kings of Israel and Judah.

E. The Faith of Jesus

An overview Jesus life according to Matthews through Acts; In looking at the Faith of Jesus, all one can do is say what the scriptures says in

> *John 21:25;*
>
> *"And there are also many other things which Jesus did, the which, if they should be written every one, I suppose that even the world itself could not contain the books that should be written. Amen."*

In order to help "Understand the Workings of Faith", Let us list some of the miracles that happen in the life of Jesus. In order for you to strengthen your faith to become strong, let's look at Faith in the life of Jesus.

According to *Matthew 14:19-21;*

> *"five loaves and two fishes, five thousand men, and left twelve baskets full;* [19]*And he commanded the multitude to sit down on the grass, and took the five loaves, and the two fishes, and looking up to heaven, he blessed, and brake, and gave the loaves to his disciples, and the disciples to the multitude.* [20]*And they did all eat, and were filled: and they took up of the fragments that remained twelve baskets full. "*[21]*And they that had eaten were about five thousand men, beside women and children."*

I have a question, how many rolls and fish do you need to feed five thousand people? If one roll feeds two people, you need 2,500 rolls to feed 5,000 men. If each person had one fish you would need 5,000 fish. If you had 25,000 people, you would need 12,500 rolls to feed them. You would need 25,000 fish to feed them.

Jesus was able to take seven loaves and the fishes, four thousand men, and left seven baskets full.

According to *Matthew 15:36-38;*

> "³⁶And he took the seven loaves and the fishes, and gave thanks, and brake them, and gave to his disciples, and the disciples to the multitude ³⁷And they did all eat, and were filled: and they took up of the broken meat that was left seven baskets full. ³⁸And they that did eat were four thousand men, beside women and children."

I have another question, how many rolls and fish do you need to feed five thousand people? If one roll feeds two people, you will need 2,000 rolls to feed 4,000 men. If each person has one fish, you will need 4,000 fish. If you have 20,000 people you will need 10,000 rolls to feed them. You will need 20,000 fish to feed them. Jesus' faith is able to bring deliverance no matter what your problem, situation, and circumstance.

According to *Matthew 10:1-3;*

> "¹And when he had called unto him his twelve disciples, he gave them power against unclean spirits, to cast them out, and to heal all manner of sickness and all manner of disease. ²Now the names of the twelve apostles are the first, Simon, who is called Peter and Andrew his brother; James the son of Zebedee, and John his brother; ³Philip, and Bartholomew; Thomas, and Matthew the publican; James the son of Alphaeus, and Lebbaeus, whose surname was Thaddaeus."

According to *John 21:24-25*;

> "²⁴This is the disciple which testifieth of these things, and wrote these things: and we know that his testimony is true. ²⁵And there are also many other things which Jesus did, the which, if they should be written every one, I suppose that even the world itself could not contain the books that should be written. Amen."

Summary

The scripture says that these are examples for our admonition according to *1 Corinthians 10:11*; "and they are written for our admonition, upon whom the ends of the world are come". We can be strong also!

Confession

PLEASE READ THIS CONFESSION ALOUD SO THAT THE OUTER EAR CAN HEAR, SO WE CAN BELIEVE SO THAT OUR FAITH WILL INCREASE. AS HUMAN BEINGS, WE PROCESS THINGS AS FOLLOWS: WE THINK IT, WE SAY IT, AND WE DO IT. BUT WITH GOD, WE KNOW THAT FAITH COMETH BY HEARING AND HEARING BY THE WORD OF GOD. WHEN WE FOLLOW THIS PRINCIPLE, WE WILL BE ABLE TO WALK IT OUT.

Jesus is the High Priest of my confession, I hold fast to my confession of faith. I decide to walk by faith and practice faith. My faith comes by hearing and hearing by the Word of God. Jesus is the author and the developer of my faith. I take my shield of faith and quench every fiery dart that the wicked one brings against me. I am a believer and not a doubter. I am the just, I live by faith, and I please my Heavenly Father. I am born of God; I have the victory over the world systems because I am a person of faith.

11. How to make your Servant Faith Strong

Many of us, as Christians, have a Servant named Faith but for many He is weak. Too many of us are living on a level with a weak servant, or level of insufficiency. Too many of us as live on the weak plateau of defeatism, because we have not risen to the plateau of faith where God means for us to live.

According to *Ephesians 6:10;*

> *"Finally, my brethren, be strong in the Lord, and in the power of his might." no one can be strong in the without being strong in faith, or having a servant that is strong in faith. In order to obtain strong faith, there are six principles. If we, as Christians, understand these six fundamentals, and if we begin to exercise and use them, we will arrive at the place where God can say to us, "You have strong faith."*

All through the Gospels, we are constantly reminded of what Jesus often had to say to His disciples.

According to *Matthew 6:30;*

> *"Wherefore, if God so clothe the grass of the field, which today is, and tomorrow is cast into the oven, shall he not much more clothe you, O ye of little faith?"*

Matthew 14:31 tells us,

> *"And immediately Jesus stretched forth his hand, and caught him, and said unto him, O thou of little faith, wherefore didst thou doubt?"*

The Bible tells us that Abraham was strong in faith. According to *Romans 4:17-21;*

> "[17](*As it is written, I have made thee a father of many nations,*) *before him whom he believed, even God, who quickeneth the dead, and calleth those things which be not as though they were.* [18]*Who against hope believed in hope, that he might become the father of many nations, according to that which was spoken, So shall thy seed be* [19]*And being not weak in faith, he considered not his own body now dead, when he was about an hundred years old, neither yet the deadness of Sarah's womb.* [20]*He staggered not at the promise of God through unbelief; but was strong in faith, giving glory to God,* [21]*And being fully persuaded that, what he had promised, he was able also to perform.*"

Faith comes from God…"Now remember that faith comes from God: Faith is a gift that God gives us at the new birth."

He gives us faith, but that faith has to be developed. It has to be matured. That faith has to be brought to a place of strength."

If we are to obtain strong faith or have a servant faith strong, then it necessary for us to learn that God's Word is real. We must know the reality of the Word of God; not to guess about it, not philosophize about it, not hope about it, but we must KNOW THE REALITY OF GOD'S WORD.

Principle Number 1
We must know the reality of God's Word. [4]

The Bible is God's Word from Genesis through Revelation. We must believe that, and practice the Word of God. GOD'S WORD IS A LIVING THING. As we continue our study on How to make our Servant Faith Strong, we realize that the Bible talks about degrees of faith.

There are degrees of Faith.

The Bible talks about weak faith; the Bible talks about strong faith; the Bible talks about great faith; the bible talks about oh ye of little faith; the Bible talks about growing faith; the Bible about unfeigned faith; and the Bible talks about shipwrecked faith. We can see from these particularly descriptive words, God has I have brought to our attention that there are degrees of faith. It is not just a matter of either having faith, or not having faith. It is a matter of us being at any given time at one level or the other.

We can possess weak faith, or we can possess strong faith. The Bible tells us that it is those who have STRONG FAITH who will obtain the promises of God. They are the ones who walk in the fullness of God's blessings. It is very important to us, that we learn the principles of strong faith.

Principle Number 2
We must know the reality of our Redemption in Christ.

Not as a creed, not as a denominational tenet, not as a traditional idea, not as some philosophical, but rather as a living reality.

In the book of Colossians, there is a very important statement that bears witness to what we are talking about.

Colossians 1:12-14:

> *"¹²Giving thanks unto the Father, which hath made us meet to be partakers of the inheritance of the saints in light: ¹³Who hath delivered us from the power of darkness, and hath translated us into the kingdom of his dear Son: ¹⁴In whom we have redemption through his blood, even the forgiveness of sins."*

Too many Christians are living a *"downstairs level of life"* in the cellar, when they should be living in the penthouse "top level style of life". If we don't live in the "penthouse", it is on us; not on God because, as we have just read, "¹²Giving thanks unto the Father, which hath made us meet to be partakers of the inheritance of the saints in light."

Until we know that as a living reality of Redemption in Christ in our life, we can never exercise strong faith. The ones who know the reality of their Redemption in Christ, and walk in light of it are the ones who have are strong faith.

Principle Number 3
We must know the reality of the New Creation. [4]

Our spirit man is the new creation. It's not our body that's new, it is our spirit man. We are a new creature in the spirit, the inner man. The spirit, the inner man, is the man that has to respond to God. God is a Spirit. Man is a spirit. He has a soul, and lives in a physical body. God deals with man through his spirit nature.

What Counts With God Is A New Creature

According Galatians 6:15;

> "*15For in Christ Jesus neither circumcision availeth anything, nor uncircumcision, but a new creature.*"

In other words, it doesn't make any difference whether we are circumcised or not circumcised as far as God is concerned. What counts with God is a new creature, a new creation. If a man is in Christ, the Word says that he is a new creature and that's what counts.

When we receive Jesus as our own personal Savior and Lord, that's how we get born again. Once we are born again we are legally the sons of God. This means that we are heirs and joint-heirs with Christ. All of the glories of heaven belong to us, because we are the living sons of God.

Until we know this as a living reality of being a new creature in Christ, we can never exercise strong faith. The ones who know the reality of their Redemption in Christ, and walk in light of it are the ones who have strong faith.

Principle Number 4
We must know the reality of our Righteousness in Christ

There are many Christians who believe in God, who believe in Christ, who go to church very regularly, who would count it the "unpardonable sin" if they didn't go to church and wouldn't feel right the rest of the week; yet, they have not learned how to exercise strong faith.

Accordingly, *1 Corinthians 1:30* says ...

> "But of him are ye in Christ Jesus, who of God is made unto Us wisdom, and <u>righteousness</u>, and sanctification, and redemption:"

Righteousness means right standing with God. That's simply what it means. It means we are right with God. Righteousness means we have a right standing with God.

It means that we on an equality with God. We have an authority and a right to stand before God and talk to Him, just as we would talk to our earthly father.

Accordingly, *2 Corinthians 5:17-21;*

> "Therefore if any man be in Christ, he is a new creature: old things are passed away; behold, all things are become new. [18]And all things are of God, who hath reconciled us to himself by Jesus Christ, and hath given to us the ministry of reconciliation; [19]To wit, that God was in Christ, reconciling the world unto himself, not imputing their trespasses unto them; and hath committed unto us the word of reconciliation. [20]Now then we are ambassadors for Christ, as though God did beseech you by us: we pray you in Christ's stead, be ye reconciled to God. [21]For he hath made him to be sin for us, who knew no sin; that we might be made the <u>righteousness of God</u> in him."

According to the Bible, not according to denominational doctrine, not according to opinion, but according to the Bible, we have been given the gift of righteousness, if we are a child of God.

COME BOLDLY TO THE THRONE OF GRACE.

Accordingly, *Hebrews 4:16;*

> "*[16]Let us therefore come boldly unto the throne of grace that we may obtain mercy, and find grace to help in time of need.*"

The verse didn't say that we are perfect or that we are righteous; therefore we have the right standing with God. This means that we can approach God and we don't have to bow our head and crawl in on our knees, or back in through the door. We can walk right up to the throne because the Bible says we can.

According to *1 John 2:1*, the word of God says,

> "*My little children, these things write I unto you, that ye sin not. And if any man sin, we have an advocate with the Father, Jesus Christ the righteous:*"

Until we know the living reality of being the <u>righteousness of God</u>, we can never exercise strong faith. The ones who know the reality of being the righteousness of God, and walk in light of it they are the ones who have are strong faith.

Principle Number 5
We must know the reality of the Indwelling Spirit. [4]

Please understand, when we talk about this principle, we are talking about those who have been filled with the Spirit. You see, every Christians is born of the spirit, but every Christians is not filled with the Holy Spirit. To be filled with to Holy Spirit doesn't save us.

We do have to be saved to be filled with the Holy Spirit, but we can be saved, born-again, and not be filled with the Holy Spirit. To be filled with the Holy Spirit is to give us supernatural power in our life. Some denominations will try to tell us, if we are not filled with the Holy Spirit and speaking in tongues, we are not saved. That's not in the biblical.

All Christians are not filled with the Spirit.

We don't have to be filled with the Holy Spirit and speak with other tongues in order to be saved, but if we are saved we can be filled with the Holy Spirit and speak with other tongues. If we are a Christian, we ought to be doing this, because God has made the Holy Spirit available to us.

If He is made available to us, He must want us to have the fullness of the Holy Spirit in our life. If we aren't filled with the Holy Spirit, apparently we are not complete, because if we were complete, we wouldn't need to be filled with the Holy Spirit.

When I say, we must know the reality of the indwelling Spirit, I am talking to those who have been filled with the Holy Spirit, who have had the experience of receiving the gift of the Holy Spirit, but they doubt it. They are not walking in the fullness of the power. They are not walking in the "supernatural"; what God expects of us. Until we know this as a living reality, we will never be able to exercise strong faith.

We read in *1 John 4:4;*

> *"⁴Ye are of God, little children, and have overcome them: because greater is he that is in you, than he that is in the world." The one that is in us or can be in us is the Holy Spirit. The one that is in the world is satan."*

The Bible is telling us that He (the Holy Spirit) that's in us, is greater than, he, Satan, that is in the world. Let me say it again, the Holy Spirit in us is more powerful and stronger than satan who is in the world.

God dwells in man by His Spirit

In *2 Corinthians 6:16*, it says...

> "¹⁶And what agreement hath the temple of God with idols? for ye are the temple of the living God; as God hath said, I will dwell in them, and walk in them; and I will be their God, and they shall be my people."

God is a Spirit, but God lives and manifests himself in and through human bodies.

This verse says ... "¹⁶And what agreement hath the temple of God with idols? For, ye are the temple of the living God; as God hath said, I will dwell IN them and walk in them."

Understanding the Working of Faith

Lend ourselves as a channel

God works through human instrumentality. He works through us. If we don't lend ourselves to Him as channels and vehicles, then He can't do anything in the earth's realm.

Don't ask me why this is true, because I don't know. I didn't make the rule. I found it when I put it into practice. I found out that it works (God's Word), so I started getting in line with it and things started happening. Thank God, we don't have to know how it works to enjoy it, to benefit from it. If we had to know how everything works we wouldn't have anything to enjoy in this life, even in the natural world.

We don't understand everything in the natural world, but we don't have to understand everything to enjoy its benefits. The scripture says that God dwells in human temples. That is, He dwells in us if we are a child of God. Again,

1 John 4:4 says…

> "⁴Ye are of God, little children, and have overcome them: because greater is he that is in you, than he that is in the world."

The one that is in you, or can be in you, is the Holy Spirit.

Temple of God

"Know ye not that ye are the temple of God, and that the Spirit of God dwelleth in you" *I Corinthians 3:16*.

Paul is telling us that God lives in us. Our bodies are the temples of God.

Rely on the Greater One.

When we realize that He is in us, we will begin to rely on the Greater One. When we begin to say to Him, "Greater One, I need a little assistance right now. I can't do it myself. I need a little power." He will put it in overdrive, press down on the passing gear, and we will have the power we need to overcome every obstacle and every temptation. We can talk to God. He is a divine person.

The Holy Spirit is the gift

God has given us His Spirit.

Isaiah 55:11;

> "Greater is He that is in me, than he that's in the world." We thank God that the Greater One lives in us today. God said, "My word shall not return to me void",

It is written, according to *Zechariah 4:6*, "Not by might, nor by power, but by my spirit, saith the Lord of Hosts."

Until we know the living reality of the Indwelling Spirit, we can never exercise strong faith. The ones who know the reality of the Indwelling Spirit, and walk in light of it they are the one who have are strong faith.

Understanding the Working of Faith

Principle Number 6
We must know the reality of Authority "Name of Jesus"

Jesus gave us authority to the body of Christ needs to understand and come to grips with the fact that there is authority in the name of Jesus. It is by that name, and through that name that we have victory, the Name of Jesus. We must know that there is authority in the Name of Jesus. We must KNOW it as a reality; we must know it, not as an idea, not as a philosophy, not as a hope, not as a dream.

We must know the reality of the authority of the name of Jesus Christ. Authority to ask or demand in the name of Jesus, Authority is of no value unless we act on it. We can have the keys to the Kingdom, but if we don't open the door, it won't do us any good. We have to open the door. The Church has this authority but it hasn't known it. It has been satisfied to feed on the fruits of emotionalism and traditionalism.

The Church has not known its rights, and the devil has taken advantage of it.

According to *John 14:12-14;*

> Jesus said..."¹²Verily, verily, I say unto you, He that believeth on me, the works that I do shall he do also; and greater works than these shall he do; because I go unto my Father. ¹³And whatsoever ye shall ask in my name, that will I do, that the Father may be glorified in the Son. ¹⁴If ye shall ask any thing in my name, I will do it."

Jesus said that we will be able to do the works that He did. We can see why we will be able to do them when we look at

Luke 10:19;

> "¹⁹Behold, I give unto you power to tread on serpents and scorpions, and over all the power of the enemy: and nothing shall by any means hurt you." He just said, "I give unto you authority over all the ability of the enemy."

That is the reason we can do the works that Jesus did. We have the authority to use His name. When we use His name, we have what is called in the legal profession, "the power of attorney." This means that when we use His name, it is as though He did it himself. We use His name and His authority in it. It is as if He himself were to use that name. *"The works that I do shall you do also."*

Authority to use the name of Jesus in prayer

Now, we want to see how the name of Jesus is used in prayer. Jesus said in *John 14:14;*

> "¹⁴If ye shall ask any thing in my name, I will do it."

When we pray, we are wasting our time if we ask Jesus for anything.

This isn't how we pray. We do not pray to Jesus. We can worship Him. We can adore Him. We can tell Him how much we love Him. We can praise His name, and all of that, but when it comes to asking for things, we have to ask the Father, in the name of Jesus.

In John chapter 15, verse 16;

> "¹⁶Ye have not chosen me, but I have chosen you, and ordained you, that ye should go and bring forth fruit, and that your fruit should remain: that whatsoever ye shall ask of the Father in my name, he may give it you. "

Jesus is telling us to ask the Father in His (Jesus') name and He (The Father) will give it you.

In *John 16:23-24;*

> Jesus said …"²³And in that day ye shall ask me nothing. Verily, verily, I say unto you, Whatsoever ye shall ask the Father in my name, he will give it us. ²⁴Hitherto have ye asked nothing in my name: ask, and ye shall receive, that your joy may be full. Jesus is saying, "Don't ask Me anything."

That is the formula for prayer. If we say that we don't know how to pray, we have just been told by Jesus. That's all there is to it. All the "thee's" and thou's" are not necessary. Jesus said, "Ask the Father for what you want, in My name, and the Father will give it to you."

Jesus snatched the keys

Jesus' name has authority in the heavens. It has authority in earth. It has authority under the earth. Jesus went down there and used that name and snatched the keys from Satan (the keys to the gates of Hades). He said, "All power in heaven and earth is in my hand." "I have the keys!" The name of Jesus is above every name.

According to *Hebrews 1:1-4*;

> "¹God, who at sundry times and in divers manners spake in time past unto the fathers by the prophets, ²Hath in these last days spoken unto us by his Son, whom he hath appointed heir of all things, by whom also he made the worlds; ³Who being the brightness of his glory, and the express image of his person, and upholding all things by the word of his power, when he had by himself purged our sins, sat down on the right hand of the Majesty on high: ⁴Being made so much better than the angels, as he hath by inheritance obtained a more excellent name than they."

When Jesus was getting ready to go back to heaven, He said, in Mark 16:17-18;

> "¹⁷And these signs shall follow them that believe; In my name shall they cast out devils; they shall speak with new tongues; ¹⁸They shall take up serpents; and if they drink any deadly thing, it shall not hurt them; they shall lay hands on the sick, and they shall recover."

He has given us authority of that NAME to break the power of Satan over our lives. Again, Principle Number Six: We must know the reality of the Authority of the Name of Jesus.

Summary

If we will master and apply these six principles, we will definitely have a servant that is strong in faith, and in return, our Servant Faith will be strong.

Confession

PLEASE READ THIS CONFESSION ALOUD SO THAT THE OUTER EAR CAN HEAR, SO WE CAN BELIEVE SO THAT OUR FAITH WILL INCREASE. AS HUMAN BEINGS, WE PROCESS THINGS AS FOLLOWS: WE THINK IT, WE SAY IT, WE DO IT. BUT WITH GOD, WE KNOW THAT FAITH COMETH BY HEARING AND HEARING BY THE WORD OF GOD. WHEN WE FOLLOW THIS PRINCIPLE, WE WILL BE ABLE TO WALK IT OUT.

Jesus is the High Priest of my confession, I hold fast to my confession of faith. I decide to walk by faith and practice faith. My faith comes by hearing and hearing by the Word of God. Jesus is the author and the developer of my faith. I take my shield of faith and quench every fiery dart that the wicked one brings against me. I am a believer and not a doubter. I am the just, I live by faith, and I please my Heavenly Father. I am born of God; I have the victory over the world systems because I am a person of faith.

12. We must see Faith as a lifestyle

As we conclude this section of the book on Faith, we want you to know that Faith is a subject on which we can teach for a year, and we still will not have exhausted or covered everything that there is to teach on the subject. The last part of this section on faith will focus on using Faith as a lifestyle.

According to *Romans 1:17;*

> "17For therein is the righteousness of God revealed from faith to faith: as it is written, The just shall live by faith."

According to *Romans 5:1-2;*

> "1Therefore being justified by faith, we have peace with God through our Lord Jesus Christ: 2By whom also we have access by faith into this grace wherein we stand, and rejoice in hope of the glory of God"

According *Romans 10:17;*

> "17So then faith cometh by hearing, and hearing by the Word of God."

God's way of asking and receiving His promises should become a way of life, therefore faith is a lifestyle.

When we receive salvation it is through faith. This becomes a new way of life for us, so we must learn and understand the law of faith. As a citizen of the Kingdom of God it is through faith that we access or claim the promises and provision of God. Christians must develop a firm foundation in the Word of God and hold fast to His promises.

Understanding the Working of Faith

Some of the keys to walking in the promises of God are as follows:

> 1) "No good thing will He withhold from those who walk uprightly", according to *Psalms 84:11*.
>
> 2) Our Heavenly Father desires His children to live by faith because it is written, "The just shall live by faith", according to *Romans 1:17*.

Faith is a law *Romans 3:27*;

> "27Where is boasting then? It is excluded. By what law? Of works? Nay: but by the law of faith."

Faith must be applied to the believer's life for healing, finances, marriage and in other areas to bring about the desired results.

Faith is the means by which you access the things of God:

According to *Romans 5:1-3*;

> "1Therefore being justified by faith, we have peace with God through our Lord Jesus Christ: 2By whom also we have access by faith into this grace wherein we stand, and rejoice in hope of the glory of God. 3And not only so, but we glory in tribulations also: knowing that tribulation worketh patience."

Some believe that faith is a wave, while others believe it is a movement. Unfortunately, Christianity has mimicked the direction of the world rather than the Scriptures.

Romans 10:17 says,

> "Faith comes by hearing and hearing by the word of God."

Understanding the Working of Faith

A) The Palsied man healed

According to *Matthew 9:2;*

> "²And, behold, they brought to him a man sick of the palsy, lying on a bed: and Jesus seeing their faith said unto the sick of the palsy; Son, be of good cheer; thy sins be forgiven thee."

B) The woman with the issue of blood

According to *Matthew 9:22;*

> "²²But Jesus turned him about, and when he saw her, he said, Daughter, be of good comfort; thy faith hath made thee whole. And the woman was made whole from that hour."

C) The Syrophenician woman's daughter

According to *Matthew 15:28;*

> "²⁸Then Jesus answered and said unto her, O woman, great is thy faith: be it unto thee even as thou wilt. And her daughter was made whole from that very hour."

D) Blind Bartimaeus's sight

According to *Mark 10:52;*

> "⁵²And Jesus said unto him, Go thy way; thy faith hath made thee whole. And immediately he received his sight, and followed Jesus in the way"

E) A blind man healed near Jericho

According to *Luke 18:42;*

> "Jesus said unto him, "Receive thy sight: thy faith hath saved thee."

Understanding the Working of Faith

A vital part of faith is the knowledge that a person must first receive it in his heart. Faith is a law, and to operate in the kingdom of God, the believer must understand how faith is activated.

God's Principles of Faith - God's principles deal with confession. Faith in God's Word comes by hearing the Word of God. Hearing the Word of God causes Faith in God and in His Word to come to you.

This spiritual force also comes out of your mouth when you speak God's Word. It actually releases God's ability to do his work in your life. I believe this is one of the reasons the Apostle Paul tells us in *Philippians 4:13*, "I can do all things through Christ which strengthens me."

Paul understood that the Word conceived inside of him and spoken out of his mouth actually set the cornerstones of his life.

Why God's Method Works - When you realize why God's method works, it makes such a difference in your attitude and increases your faith.

Why is creative power released inside you when you speak God's Word out of your mouth? This is essentially what God told Joshua under the Old Covenant.

According to *Joshua 1:8;*

> "This book of the law shall not depart out of thy mouth; but thou shalt meditate therein day and night, that thou mayest observe to do according to all that is written therein: for then thou shalt make thy way prosperous, and then thou shalt have good success."

Do you want to make your way prosperous? Do you want to know the key, the secret of being successful in life? It is to do exactly what God told Joshua to do.

PUT THE WORD OF GOD IN YOUR MOUTH. SPEAK IT OUT DAY AND NIGHT; DO NOT LET IT DEPART FROM YOUR MOUTH!

Allow me share with you why this principle is so important. The words you speak are more important to you than to anyone else. The reason your words are so important to you, is they affect you more than they affect anyone else. This is why it is vital to speak blessings and not curses!!

The individual who speaks negative words, whether they are cursing someone, using the Lord's name in vain, griping, or mumbling and complaining is not hurting someone else, but he/she is actually hurting him/herself.

He is actually bringing negativity and curses upon himself by speaking negative words. Have you ever been around someone who had a negative vibe or energy? Of course, we all have. And by the words of his mouth he was a toxic creature. By having negative thought waves, we can actually cause toxicity to build up in our bodies. Keeping ourselves guarded and surrounded by positive people and energy is essential in our healing.

The old saying, "what goes around comes around", has been proven to be very true!! And by the same token, we are not to judge others as it states in

In *Matthew Chapter 7:1-2;*

> "¹Judge not, that ye be not judged. ²For with what judgment ye judge, ye shall be judged: and with what measure ye mete, it shall be measured to you again."

This is why it is crucial to speak positive words towards others, even your enemies, since negative words hurt only you. The inner ear feeds your voice directly into the human spirit....what is referred to as the heart.

That is why the words you speak are more important to you than anyone else. The words you speak affect your entire being. Spirit Soul and Body!

Jesus knew this principle two thousand years ago as He only spoke and taught of the things of God. In Mark 9:23, ²³Jesus said unto him, If thou canst believe, all things are possible to him that believeth.

In *Mark 11:23-24;*

> ²³For verily I say unto you, That whosoever shall say unto this mountain, Be thou removed, and be thou cast into the sea; and shall not doubt in his heart, but shall believe that those things which he saith shall come to pass; he shall have whatsoever he saith. ²⁴Therefore I say unto you, what things soever ye desire, when ye pray, believe that ye receive them, and ye shall have them."

Planting Seed of Faith - Speaking what God says does several things. When you speak the Word out of your mouth, you are planting a seed. The more you speak the Word, the more you believe it. The more you believe the Word, the more you speak it.

In *2 Corinthians 4:13* we find these words,

> "We, having the same spirit of faith, according as it is written, I believed, and therefore have I spoken; we also believe, and therefore speak."

The Apostle Paul was quoting an Old Testament Scripture, according to *Psalm 116:10;*

> "I believed, therefore have I spoken Then he said We also believe, and therefore speak."

This principle initiates the process. It's in your mouth, and it's in your heart. When it's in your heart in abundance, it gets in your mouth. "Out of the abundance of the heart the mouth speaketh."

I can always tell where people are, in their spiritual walk, by the words they speak. That which is abundant in their heart always shows up in their mouth. Have you ever heard this statement being applied to individuals, "they are emotionally draining?" Their negative words rub off on you, and your spirit and theirs are not in harmony. They drain your positive flow! So...if you are in need of a healing in your body, DO NOT subject yourself to negative speaking individuals who drain your positive thinking and positive words. By their words....they are planting seeds of doubt!!

Our spirit, our heart is the production center of our bodies. This is where the kingdom of God resides. It dwells inside you. This is where Jesus dwells in the person of the Holy Spirit.

This kingdom dwells within you! It is capable of producing everything that you plant! You can either plant positive seeds...which are God's law of Faith...His Word, or you can plant negative seeds of fear and doubt. It is your choice! I praise God that He opened my mind and spirit to His Truths concerning my healing. It wasn't until I began meditating on God's promises regarding healing or whatever my needs, and I began speaking His Word, did I begin to see a change!

Summary

Believers must understand how to operate by faith. To operate by faith does not make sense to the natural man. When Christians rely on sense knowledge only, they are robbed of revelation knowledge from God.

Confession

PLEASE READ THIS CONFESSION ALOUD SO THAT THE OUTER EAR CAN HEAR, SO WE CAN BELIEVE SO THAT OUR FAITH WILL INCREASE. AS HUMAN BEINGS, WE PROCESS THINGS AS FOLLOWS: WE THINK IT, WE SAY IT, WE DO IT. BUT WITH GOD, WE KNOW THAT FAITH COMETH BY HEARING AND HEARING BY THE WORD OF GOD. WHEN WE FOLLOW THIS PRINCIPLE, WE WILL BE ABLE TO WALK IT OUT.

Jesus is the High Priest of my confession, I hold fast to my confession of faith. I decide to walk by faith and practice faith. My faith comes by hearing and hearing by the Word of God. Jesus is the author and the developer of my faith. I take my shield of faith and quench every fiery dart that the wicked one brings against me. I am a believer and not a doubter. I am the just, I live by faith, and I please my Heavenly Father. I am born of God; I have the victory over the world systems because I am a person of faith.

13. FAITH DECLARATIONS

MAKEAKE FAITH DECLARATIONS; WHO I AM, WHAT I HAVE, AND WHAT I CAN DO!

<u>MONDAY</u> - I WALK IN LOVE AND FAITH

- **Jesus is Lord** over my spirit, my soul, and my body;
- I Thank You Heavenly Father that your love has been shed abroad in my heart by the Holy Spirit and that your love abides in me richly;
- Heavenly Father, I Love You, with all my heart, with all my soul, with all my strength, and with all my money-might;
- I Love my neighbor as myself.
- Heavenly Father, I thank you, that I am filled with YOUR fullness.
- I am rooted and grounded in Love;
- I keep myself in the Kingdom of light, in Love, in the Word, and the wicked one touches me not;
- I am a spirit, I have a soul, I live in a physical body;
- I am in the world, but I am not of this world;
- I am born of the Spirit, and filled with the Spirit of God, and I am led by the Spirit of God;
- I trust in the Lord, with all of my heart and I lean not to my own understanding;
- In all my ways I acknowledge Him, and He directs my paths. My pathway is life and not death;
- I walk in the light of the Word of God;
- Heavenly Father, Your WORD is lamp unto my feet;
- Heavenly Father, Your WORD is a light unto my path;
- Heavenly Father, your WORD is food unto my spirit;
- Heavenly Father, Your Word shall not depart out of my mouth.

TUESDAY - I FLOW IN THE GUIDANCE OF THE HOLY SPIRIT

- **Heavenly Father**, Please don't Let me miss you today, use me every day in a mighty way. Let me sense your presence and your fresh renewal every day of my life;
- I thank you for the memories of yesterday, but I need to experience you today, I am expecting great things from you tomorrow. Yesterday is gone, but today and tomorrow I live in expectation of a new and wonderful outpouring of your Mighty Spirit in my life;
- I am born of the Spirit, filled with the Spirit of God;
- The Holy Spirit dwells within me;
- The Spirit of truth abideth in me and teaches me all things and guides me into all truths;
- I am what Word of God says I am;
- I can do what the Word of God says I can do;
- I have what the Word of God says I have;
- I am a spirit, I have a soul, and I live in a physical body;
- I am in the world, but I am not of this world;
- I am made in God's image;
- I have God's nature on the inside of me;
- I have God's ability within me through Christ;
- I am working together with Christ;
- Gods plan is for me to go forth in His ability and power;
- I am bold, I am courageous, I am a strong person;
- God is my Father, He is for me, who can be against me;
- Holy Spirit, You are my counselor; Teaching me, educating me, training me, and develop my human spirit;
- Greater is He that is in me than he that is in the world;
- The Holy Spirit dwells within me.

WEDNESDAY - I WALK IN THE MIRACLE WORKING POWER OF GOD

- **Heavenly Father**, Thank You for Your mercy and grace.
- I am born-again; I am filled with the Holy Spirit.
- I am a supernatural being, filled with the supernatural power of God;
- I am made in the image of God;
- Through the Holy Spirit within me, I have the same miracle-working power that Christ has, to do the same mighty works He did;
- I am a believer and I am expecting His miracle power to be released within me to meet the desperate needs of those around me;
- Thank you that you are releasing your miracle power and other are being minister unto in spirit, soul and body by your Spirit and through your WORD.
- I meditate promises day and night;
- I shall make way prosperous;
- I will have good success in life;
- I am a doer of Your Word and put Your Word first;
- I center everything around the WORD of God;
- I am a believer and not a doubter;
- I hold fast to my confession of faith;
- I decide to walk by faith and practice faith;
- My faith comes by hearing
- Hearing by the Word of God;
- Jesus is the author and the developer of my faith;
- I take my shield of faith
- I quench fiery dart that the wicked one brings against me;
- I am the just, I live by faith, I please my Heavenly Father.

THURSDAY - I AM HEALED AND HAVE MY PHYSICAL NEEDS MET

- **Heavenly Father,** I bless you and I love you;
- I bless and love my enemies;
- I forgive them now and I release them in the name of Jesus;
- Christ has redeemed from every sickness written in the curse of the law;
- I am redeemed from every disease that is not written in the book of the law;
- Christ has redeemed me, brought me back and set me FREE from all sickness and diseases;
- I have been delivered from the authority of darkness;
- In Christ Jesus I have redemption;
- I have been ransom from captivity;
- I am delivered from satan dominion and his work;
- I am free from sickness and disease;
- I am healed;
- I am a member of the Body of Christ;
- I am redeemed from the curse, because Jesus bore my sickness and carried my diseases in His own body. By His stripes I am healed;
- I forbid any sickness or disease to operate in my body;
- Every organ, every tissue of my body functions in the perfection in which God created it to function;
- I honor God and bring glory to Him in my body.

FRIDAY - ALL MY MATERIAL AND FINANCIAL NEEDS ARE PROVIDED

- Jesus has destroyed the curse over my life;
- Christ has redeemed me from the curse of the law;
- For poverty He has given me wealth;
- I am prosperous, rich, and wealthy;
- I am out of debt and all my needs are met;
- I have plenty more to put in store;
- I sow bountifully; I reap bountifully;
- I am attracting your blessing like a magnet;
- I am full of Joy, full of life, I am Healed, I am Debt free;
- Lord I acknowledge you this day;
- You have sent your angels unto me to walk with me;
- Angels walk in front of me to prepare my way; they walk behind me to protect me from area that I cannot see;
- Angels walk beside me for comfort and company;
- Angels are with me today;
- Where ever I go is prosperous;
- I am prosperous in every area of my life;
- Everything I put my hands to prosper;
- The world must make way for me; because (**Your Name**) in the Lord Jesus Christ, as an ambassador of the Kingdom of God is coming through; Fear not, God is my shield, Abundant compensation, and my reward shall be exceedingly great!
- I will never worry about where my next meal is going to come from, or the next meal for my family;
- My kitchen cabinets, refrigerators, and freezers are full;
- I have all the resource that is necessary to live a life fill with abundance.

SATURDAY - TO WALK IN THE FAVOR AND WISDOM OF GOD

- **Heavenly Father**, I thank you because you are doing exceedingly abundantly above all that I can ask or Think Your mighty power is taking over in me;
- I am an heir of God through Jesus Christ; I am a joint-heir with Jesus Christ;
- I let the word of God dwell in me richly; He who began a good work in me will continue until the day of Christ;
- I have perfect knowledge of every situation and every circumstance that I come up against. Jesus has been made unto me wisdom, righteousness, sanctification, and redemption;
- I have the wisdom of God, I am the righteousness of God in Christ Jesus;
- I am sanctified and sealed by the Holy Spirit;
- I am the redeemed of the Lord;
- I have an abundance of Favor flowing from God to me
- I am a success today, I have God's special favor upon me I am someone very special to my Heavenly Father, and nothing is impossible with Him today; His favor is upon me today;
- I think like it, I live like it, I drive like it, I dress like it;
- I am expecting great things to happen in my life today;
- I obtained favor in the sight of all who look upon me;
- I will meet nice people today;
- I shall have good relationships with people today;
- I shall favor and honor others today;
- I am a blessing to the Lord. I am a blessing to others;
- Lord Jesus, You are my Lord and my Savior.

SUNDAY - I WALK IN THE BLESSING

- **Heaven Father**, I Thank You that I am blessed because I am born into BLESSING;
- Thank you that the blessing is working in me, on me, and around me;
- I declare that I am blessed when I come in and I am blessed when I go out;
- Jesus came to the earth to restore the blessing that Adam lost in the Garden of Eden when he sinned;
- I am a child of God. I have a covenant right to the blessing;
- I declare that like Abraham I am blessed to be a blessing until all the families of the earth are blessed, the blessing of God is on my life;
- I am empowered to prosper in every endeavor that I take on and every project that I begin;
- I am blessed on my job;
- I am blessed in all my relationships. Like Joseph, those in authority over me see the blessing of God on my life;
- I have favor as a result. Thanks for blessing me with all spiritual blessings in heavenly places;
- I am powerful, wealthy, influential and blessed! In Jesus Name Amen.

Scriptures References

1 John 5:4:
1 Timothy 6:12
2 Corinthians 4:13
2 Corinthians 4:18
2 King 5:1-4, 8 -14
2 Kings 4:26
2 Kings 5:1–15
2 Timothy 1:7
Acts 14:7-10
Deuteronomy 8:18
Ephesians 6:13
Genesis 17:3-5
Hebrew 11:6
Hebrews 10:23
Hebrews 11:1
Isaiah 55:11
James 1:22
James 1:5, 7
Jeremiah 1:12
John 14:12
John 20:19-29
John 9:6-7
Joshua 6:1-16, 20
Luke 1:5-20
Luke 22:32
Luke 7:1-9
Luke 8:25
Mark 10:52
Mark 11:23
Mark 4:36-40;
Mark 5:34

1 Peter 3:4
2 Corinthians 2:11
2 Corinthians 4:13-15
2 Corinthians 5:7;
2 Kings 4: 8-37
2 Kings 4:35-37
2 Kings 6:12-17
Acts 11:13-14
Acts 8:5-8
Ephesians 2:8-9:
Genesis 1:1-26
Habakkuk 2:2-4
Hebrews 1:14
Hebrews 10:35-37
Hebrews 11:1-4
Isaiah 55:8-11
James 1:23,24
James 2:17
John 10:10
John 2:1-11
John 4:24
Joshua 1:8
Luke 1:20
Luke 18:42
Luke 5:1-9
Luke 7:36-50
Luke 7:1-9
Mark 11:22-24;
Mark 4:35-41
Mark 5:25-34
Mark 9:23

Understanding the Working of Faith

Mark 11:19-22	Mark 11:22-24
Matthew 12:9-13	Matthew 14:24-31
Matthew 14:30	Matthew 15:22-28
Matthew 15:28	Matthew 16:7-12
Matthew 17:20	Matthew 6:25-33
Matthew 7:1-2	Matthew 8:23-26
Matthew 9:2	Matthew 9:22
Matthew 9:27-31	Matthew: 9:27-29
Matthew; 14:22-31	Philippians 4:13
Philippians 4:6	Proverb 18:21
Proverbs 13:22	Psalms 103:20-21;
Psalms 116:10	Psalms 35:27
Psalms 84:11	Romans 1:16-17
Romans 1:17	Romans 10:17
Romans 10:8 -14	Romans 10:9-10 (NTL)
Romans 12:3	Romans 3:27
Romans 5:1-2	Romans 5:1-3

Heavenly Decision

To receive Jesus Christ as your own personal Lord and Savior

Are you born again? Have you ever received Jesus as your Lord and Savior? If the answer to this question is no, read these scriptures and pray this prayer, agreeing with it and believing it from your heart

John 3:16 "For God so loved the world, that he gave his only begotten Son, that whosoever believeth in him should not perish, but have everlasting life"

Romans 10:9-10, 13 "That if thou shalt confess with thy mouth the Lord Jesus, and shalt believe in thine heart that God hath raised him from the dead, thou shalt be saved. For whosoever shall call upon the name of the Lord shall be saved. For with the heart man believeth unto righteousness; and with the mouth **Confession** is made unto salvation.

Pray this pray now: Salvation

Dear God,

I want to become a citizen of your Kingdom. I come to you in the name of Jesus, your son. I confess I am a sinner. I believe you sent your son to die on the cross for my sins. I confess with my mouth that Jesus Christ is Lord. Thank you for allowing me to become a Christian; I am translated from the kingdom of darkness to the Kingdom of God.

In Jesus' name I pray, Amen!

Understanding the Working of Faith

As a genuine born-again Christian, a citizen of the Kingdom of God wants, above everything else, to do the will of God. Don't be ashamed to witness to others and tell them how to become a Christian. Join a Bible believing Church and be water baptized as an act of faith to let the world know you are following Christ's example.

Signed _____ Date _____

If you would like to receive the Holy Spirit, ask the Father in Jesus' name to fill you with the Holy Spirit. Believe you receive when you ask, and begin to speak your new language in faith as God gives it to you.

Pray this pray now: Receive the fullness of the Holy Spirit

Heavenly Father,

I come to you in faith, believing that Jesus Christ died in my place, for my sins, and arose from the dead. I ask you to fill me to overflowing with the Holy Spirit. You said in your Word that if I asked I would receive, so I ask you now to fill me to overflowing with your precious Holy Spirit. I receive Him now by faith and expect to speak with other tongues as he gives me the utterance. In Jesus' Name Amen

Pray this pray now: Receive healing

Now I want you to pray for your healing. Put your hand on your body where you are sick and repeat this prayer: Lord Jesus you are the Great Physician. All healing comes from you. By your stripes we are healed. I speak your Word over this body and thank you that you heal all our diseases. Thank you for healing and enabling me to walk in health. In Jesus' Name Amen

Endnotes

1. Bible, King James Vision (1997) containing the Old Testament and New Testament Authorized King James Version Red-Letter, Illinois: Tyndale House Publication
2. Bible Faith Study Course By Kenneth E. Hagin
3. Ever Increasing Faith By Smith Wiggles Worth
4. How to obtain strong Faith By Frederick K. C. Price

About the Author

Pastor James L. Monteria is born again. He was called into the ministry and ordained by Faith Christian Fellowship, International of Tulsa, Oklahoma. To effectively execute the call on his life, he attended Rhema Bible Training Center of Broken Arrow a suburb of Tulsa, Oklahoma where he earned a Diploma in Ministerial Training.

Pastor Monteria received his Bachelor's of Science Degree in Business Administration from Saint Paul's College in Lawrenceville, VA. He received a Master's Degree in Instructional Education from Central Michigan University, Mount Pleasant, Michigan.

Pastor Monteria has ministered the Word of God through seminars, church services, Bible studies, Prison Ministries, distribution of his books CD's and DVD's. Pastor Monteria believes that the Bible is the Word of God, and he is an anointed Pastor and Teacher of the Word of God. His ministries are combinations of anointed Preaching and Teaching the Word of God; and flowing in the gifts of the Holy Spirit as the lead.

Pastor J. L. Monteria is available for:
~Speaking Engagements~
~Book Signings~
~Workshops\Conferences~
You may contact J L Monteria for other books by Pastor J L Monteria, please
Visit our Website: www.clmpublication.info
Email: clmpublication.info@gmail.com
Postal Mailing: P.O. Box 932 Chesterfield, Va 23832

www.ingramcontent.com/pod-product-compliance
Lightning Source LLC
Chambersburg PA
CBHW070811100426
42742CB00012B/2329